Praise for

The Thing About Work
and Richard A. Moran

"*The Thing About Work* stands alone. Moran's new book combines spot-on advice with humor, in essays that nail the complexities of today's workplace. You will recognize the people and places in this book and smile at the situations in which we find ourselves. Without judgment, Moran tells us how to deal with these situations. Read it, smile, and be more successful."

—Zarine Khara, founder and CEO of JustGiving

"Rich Moran offers common sense—but seldom implemented—practical tips for succeeding at work. At once insightful and humorous, *The Thing About Work* nails current foibles and behaviors that get people fired, as well as the behaviors that lead to success."

—Jeffrey Pfeffer, Thomas D. Dee II professor of Organizational Behavior, Graduate School of Business, Stanford University, and author of *Leadership BS*

"Rich Moran's *The Thing About Work* perfectly captures the follies, routines, craziness, and complexities of the modern workplace, and it does so with such uncanny accuracy that you'd think he was writing about your organization—or even you! It is workplace humor at its best—riotously funny, spot-on social criticism. And yet, you can tell that deep down Rich loves work, workplaces, and the people in them. He just wants us to be our best selves there. If you want to know how to do that, you'll also find that on every page. This is Rich Moran's best book yet, and I highly recommend you read it. More than once."

—Jim Kouzes, Dean's Executive Fellow of Leadership, Leavey School of Business, Santa Clara University, and coauthor of *The Leadership Challenge*

"*The Thing About Work* is a crafty view of modern work with recipes for success and unfortunately gotcha's for failure. Rich again, captures in bite-size chunks real-world workplace wisdom told in a humorous way that everyone can identify with, either in themselves and certainly others. *The Thing About Work* should be required reading for all college graduating seniors preparing their first résumé."

—Ray A. Rothrock, chair and CEO, RedSeal, Inc., partner emeritus Venrock, and former chair of the National Venture Capital Association

"I have long been an admirer of Moran's work as a leader, consultant, and a writer. His unique books always contain important insights about people and the contemporary workplace, combining wisdom and practical guidance with compelling anecdotes. Working in the opera field as I do, which is known for its unique personnel situations on, and off, the stage, I find Moran's guidance both invaluable and entertaining."

—Keith Cerny, PhD, Kern Wildenthal general director & CEO, the Dallas Opera

"Everything you need to know about work—how to stand out, how to sound like an idiot, how to maneuver, and how to get ahead. You will laugh out loud at how Moran captures the essence of the workplace in memorable, pithy descriptions that will stick with you forever."

—Lee Caraher, CEO, Double Forte, author of *Millennials & Management: The Essential Guide to Making it Work at Work*

"Although we spend more than half our waking hours doing work, most of us neglect to reflect upon what is actually going on at work. Rich Moran's witty and empathetic books help us all put life in the workplace in perspective, and this one is his best yet."

—Geoffrey Moore, author of *Crossing the Chasm*

the
Thing
about
Work

the Thing *about* Work

SHOWING UP AND OTHER IMPORTANT MATTERS

Richard A. Moran

bibliomotion
inc.

First published by Bibliomotion, Inc.

39 Harvard Street

Brookline, MA 02445

Tel: 617-934-2427

www.bibliomotion.com

Printed in the United States of America

Print ISBN 978-1-62956-158-5

E-book ISBN 978-1-62956-159-2

Enhanced E-book ISBN 978-1-62956-160-8

CIP data has been applied for.

This book is dedicated to all those who show up each and every day to do the best they can and apply common sense to complex problems; and to C.

Contents

Special Holiday Bonus Section

Introduction

The thing about work is that we love it; we hate it; we need it; we miss it; we talk about it all the time; we measure ourselves by it; we judge others by it; we are addicted to it. Work might define us and it might fulfill us. Why does a CEO who has already made hundreds of millions of dollars continue to work? Why does a rock star who has made a bundle continue to tour? Why do we all wrestle with our life's work? Why do retirees miss work as soon as they stop doing it? How do we deal with work as the technology changes, millennials take over, and organizations grapple to set new guidelines?

Definitive answers are hard to come by since there is so much change going on in the workplace, but there are some guidelines and directions that apply. Through essays, stories, and prescriptions, I hope to bring some clarity to the workplace and show how to not just survive but thrive.

Why buy business books? Lots of new books that preach about weight loss are published each year. Yet, we all sort of know that losing weight is a matter of eating right and getting exercise. Everything else is on the fringe. But we all buy the diet books with keen anticipation.

Business books are the same way. Thousands are published each year. But we all know that success in business is about setting a strategy, executing on that strategy, and measuring results. There are no secrets, but we are all looking for simple answers. Any edge and new idea could be all we need.

I hate to be the one to break the news, because I write business books. There are very few shortcuts and even fewer secrets about success in business. The best business book ever written might be the one you heard from your mother—work hard and do the right thing. Everything else is a bonus.

My journey in business book writing began accidentally.

"You remind me of a golden retriever!" With that simple statement my pursuit of writing business books began.

The woman made the statement to me with all the sincerity and enthusiasm of someone who had made a new discovery. It was, in fact, a time of discovery: it was a job interview and she was the candidate. She continued to gush, "No, really. You have the same enthusiasm as a golden, you even have the same coloring!" It was hard to know how to respond. Should I bark? Wag my tail? Drool?

She was an excellent candidate and was being considered for a very senior role in which she would make a lot of money. Two of us were interviewing her but I was the one who looked like a dog. At the end of the interview, my colleague asked me, "Do you think we should give someone a job who told you that you look like a dog?" The answer was no.

Later that same day I was guiding a client through a critical presentation to a financial crowd. It was the group that could upgrade or downgrade a company's prospects and the stock price would move accordingly. My client, the presenter, had a lot to say and had prepared a lengthy PowerPoint presentation. He was sure of his work and before he showed each slide he proudly proclaimed, "I know you can't read this, BUT..." (I am going to show you anyway). That phrase is an invitation to not pay attention. No one did. By the second slide he introduced that way, the audience had taken out their devices and were checking e-mail, texting, and even chatting on the phone. The presenter, who earned more than a million dollars a year, looked puzzled that no one was paying attention.

Even later that same day, now in the afternoon, I was joining the head of marketing for a hot tech company. The company was introducing a new product and the marketing head was explaining it to the advertising agency, the PR firm, and the internal marketing team. The median age of the audience was thirty, and 90 percent of the audience was attractive women. The product was cool and the presenter was hip, or thought he was, wearing blue jeans and a black shirt. But there was a problem—the shirt did not fit.

It is true that none of us weighs what we did in college, and he definitely did not. The buttons on his shirt bowed and swelled and created little white half-moons between each button. Unfortunately, he was not wearing a T-shirt and his hairy belly stuck out.

The audience was rapt, not listening to his presentation but staring at the buttons and his belly with anticipation. When he turned away from the audience, eyes rolled and fingers were stuck down throats in mock gagging mechanisms. The new product was lost. His credibility with the group was lost over a shirt that didn't fit.

Still the same day, at JFK airport while waiting for my flight to San Francisco, I witnessed a young bucko business guy berate the gate agent with f-bombs and worse. The agent was unable to upgrade our abusive traveler and he was enraged. He invoked his billion-miles-flown status and the fact that his investment banking firm was a major customer and he was a special guy to an increasingly disinterested agent. The more he screamed, the calmer the gate agent became because she had called security. Not only was he not upgraded; he was thrown off the flight altogether. He might still be at the same airport jail. He never learned that there is an inverse relationship between yelling and first-class seats.

My day in New York had now ended and I jumped on a six-hour flight with a set of questions like:

- Is it me who is out of step or am I the only one left in business with common sense? Do people not know that there are simple rules to follow to be successful?
- Why do I need to tell people not to tell the interviewer that he looks like a dog? Or that they should show slides that people can read and wear clothes that fit and be polite to airline people?

Turns out, people are looking for simple when it comes to rules for success and coping with the workplace, and they are looking for the truth. Navigating through the worlds of work and family and all the white space surrounding those two big categories is stressful and demanding and growing more difficult. If truth and humor improve our chances to survive and, dare I say it, enjoy work, then I am a big success.

The essays and stories here are derived from countless meetings, airplane trips, interviews, staff retreats, and just showing up. I sometimes think that business books are really three bullets of advice that are stretched out to three hundred pages. So to whet your appetite, here are my three bullets:

- ■ **RULE:** Tell the truth about what is really happening in the organization so that people can work on the right things.
- ■ **RULE:** If you don't like your boss, you will never like your job. Think change.
- ■ **RULE:** *Never* answer your cell phone while in the bathroom. We are supposed to be in charge of technology, not vice versa.

My message is that work isn't so bad and there are ways to make it better. We all feel most fulfilled when we are productive at work. There are lots of things—some big, some not—that we can all do to improve our lives at work. If we can laugh along the way, that's even better. And that is what this book is all about. There are some things about work too simple not to know.

And sometimes work is an unexpected adventure that can lead to new ideas. A scene from another trip to New York was one of those adventures, summarized here in a letter to the CFO:

Dear CFO:

I apologize in advance for not having a receipt for a $50 taxi ride. I believe I have a good reason, as follows:

Recently, the Atlanta GM and I decided to share a taxi from midtown Manhattan to two airports. We had participated in critical sales meetings that day. The Atlanta GM was departing from New York's LaGuardia and I from JFK, which is way farther out. The taxi dropped her at LGA and the driver insisted I pay him then for that segment because all trips to airports are flat rates. I paid him the $38 and we set off for JFK. In order to get back on the Long Island Expressway the driver had to get on a side street, where the taxi stalled and he pulled over.

Just as the driver was able to restart the cab, a black SUV pulled in front of us, blocking the taxi. The SUV's driver asked if my driver could take somebody to JFK. The passenger in the SUV got out, a diminutive young African American man. My driver said okay, and asked me if it was okay. Sensing a Good Samaritan chance, I said okay too. At that point, another young guy got out of the SUV who might have been three hundred pounds and was not smiling.

We hit it off famously. At JFK my new friends were set to depart on Delta, the first stop. Mr. Big said he would "take care of it" and I saw him give the driver $40 cash for a $35 meter. We shook hands all around and promised to be friends on FB.

Five minutes later we arrived at the United terminal. I was rushing to get out of the taxi when the barely English-speaking driver told me I owed him $50. I said, "No way, the other guy paid you," and removed my bag as he went yelling for an NYPD cop. The driver showed the cop the meter and I explained my side. The cop said, "Give him $25.00 and move on." I gave him the cash, we exchanged f-bombs, and I entered the United terminal. I didn't ask for a receipt since the driver was still yelling at me in an unknown language. He was not wishing me a safe trip. Upon entering the terminal I realized that, in the heat of battle, I'd left my cell phone in the back of the taxi.

I went back to the curb and, as I suspected, the taxi driver had made a circle to come back with the phone. He stopped traffic, held up the phone, and yelled, "Twenty-five bucks and it's yours." I gave him the cash and once again felt it inappropriate to request a receipt.

By now I had cut it really close to make my flight. I made it but just barely, and as a result I lost my reserved seat and was reseated in row 39B, middle, near the lavatory, for the six-hour flight.

I hope you will understand my problem with the receipt.

Sincerely,

Richard A. Moran, Chief Executive Officer

And the book about "things" at work began again with a new rule: Never leave a taxi (or Uber) without double-checking the whereabouts of your cell phone.

The Thing About the Refrigerator

Go to any workplace with a break room or a kitchen tucked away in the corner of the office. There, between the coffee canisters, the bucket of red licorice, and the salty snacks, is the big refrigerator. And taped there on the refrigerator door is a sign that says something like... THIS REFRIG-ERATOR WILL BE CLEANED ON FRIDAY AT 4:00. EVERYTHING (OTHER THAN SALAD DRESSING) WILL BE TOSSED. Signed, THE HIRED HELP.

And Friday at 4:00 the refrigerator will be cleaned out and everything, save salad dressing, is, in fact, tossed. It's a gross and rotten job but that act of cleaning the refrigerator is the one thing that all organizations can count on to be implemented, and implementation is what success is all about. A plan that is implemented is successful. A strategy that is executed is a success. A project that is completed is a success. The best implementation example in the organization is right there in front of us, hanging on the refrigerator. Okay, that is an easy one, but if we remember that simple lesson and use it as a metaphor, we will all be more successful.

Where the Rubber Meets the Air

Certain phrases that are part of the workplace are just too good not to use. These are not phrases from management like, "people are our most important asset" or "changing the paradigm on client engagement." Certain phrases capture the essence of what's going on in the organization so perfectly that further explanation is never needed. The best phrases don't come out of the CEO's office, or from consultants, or off of the framed vision statement on the wall. The best phrases come out of the bowels of the organization. Management may not even know they exist.

The most creative and cut-to-the-heart-of-the-matter phrases all seem to have something to do with getting things done. Call it implementation, call it execution, call it program management or change management—the name doesn't matter. The inability to get things done generates good phrases.

Here are five of my favorites, all from people who do real work.

- **Rotating bald tires.** Or, wow, this is hard work but all this effort will go nowhere, and in the end nothing will change. When you rotate bald tires, you still have four bald tires.
- **We are building our own coffin.** This phrase means we are doing a lot of work and the result will be that we are out of a job. This phrase usually comes from project teams involved in cutting costs.
- **Mushroom management.** This was described to me as when you are treated like a mushroom, that is, kept in the dark and fed, well, we will call it fertilizer. I know exactly what that means.
- **Same old horses, same old glue.** Or, the same people will always generate the same result. This applies when cost cutting means all the low-paid people are eliminated but no one whose photo is on the organization chart.
- And my favorite: **Where the rubber meets the air.** Meaning, the wheel never hits the ground—the opposite of "where the rubber meets the road." All the talk is good but nothing will ever get implemented. It's the plan du jour that provides no hope of making a difference.

Lots of other phrases circulate through a workplace but most are not suitable for print. With so much going on in the workplace, why does the inability to get things done generate so much creativity in the catchphrase department? The answer is simple: FRUSTRATION. Nothing will make a team or an individual more frustrated than the sense of working on something that will never get implemented, that nothing will ever change.

Execution of a plan is the most difficult activity of any organization. Strategies and plans can be copied. Who cares? Effective implementation is the secret sauce in any organization, and requires discipline and hard decisions. It is so difficult because it requires changing behaviors, which most people don't want to do. It requires changing out people—and it depends on which side of that change you are on, but most people don't want to see change in this regard. It requires making difficult decisions that are by their nature tough to make. Implementation requires courage, which can be hard to come by in some leadership ranks.

Strategies are necessary. Plans are required. Goal setting is critical. Lists of things to do are important and necessary. But the success of any individual or organization is measured in what has been accomplished, not in what was planned.

I do know that where there is effective implementation, phrases are not necessary because results don't require phrases. And people generally like their jobs more.

Be alert to the phrase du jour at work, it may tell you more than you think.

The Saddest Three Letters in Business

Acronyms have created a new language, and we all speak that new language. Some letter phrases are so widely held that we use them in speaking. Phrases like LOL, FYI, and BTW are second nature. Others are not as widely used, like @TEOTD (At the End of the Day) or YKW-YCD (You Know What You Can Do), but even those are creeping into the language.

Each one captures a sentiment in a few letters that is both direct and efficient. And somehow the group of letters doesn't seem as bad as the hackneyed buzzwords. Twitter and the constant barrage of instant messages have helped create the new language. It is ever expanding and here to stay AFAIK (As Far As I Know).

But there is one rarely used three-letter designation that can kill a career. Sometimes it is not used explicitly but it is always there, lurking in conference rooms and project plans. The worst three letters in business that can be assigned to your name are: D N F.

DNF stands for DID NOT FINISH. Anyone who ever enters a race knows those three unfortunate letters. Whether the race is running, swimming, bike riding, or Formula One racing, it doesn't matter. When the results are posted, DNF next to your name means you started something but didn't finish. And in a race, just like any project, one either finishes or does not. Swimming halfway across the English Channel doesn't count as swimming across the English Channel. It means DNF, Did Not Finish.

At the office the DNF letters may not be placed next to any name. But the label exists. The DNF label means you start things and that is as far as you got. It means you are good at thinking but not at doing. It probably means no one wants to work with you and it could mean you will be out of a job. You may think others don't notice or that it is NBD (No Big Deal). It is a big deal and should be avoided.

Don't be caught in the DNF box. It's more important to tackle projects that you know you can finish than it is to start huge projects that everyone knows will never be completed. The BHAG (Big Hairy Audacious Goal) can be tempting but don't make the goal so hairy that it will never be achieved.

Sometimes you don't have a choice of assignments, but always avoid the dreaded DNF label. Crossing the finish line is a very good feeling.

GFN (Gone for Now).

The "At the End of the Day" Thing

The end of the day happens every day. It is predictable. But the phrase "at the end of the day" is so ubiquitous that it seems to be news that each day ends. Politicians use it, children use it, but most of all, people who are working use it.

I think it means, "When all is said and done." Or, it could mean, "I know what I am talking about and you don't." Or, it could mean, "Shut up, the decision is made." The end of the day is now all day long.

The irony is that, given the technology and workloads that never end, there *is* no end of the day. At the end of the day, there still is, "It is what it is…" which is even worse. The "it is what it is" phrase implies "give up." It often sounds like, "life sucks and work is even worse." Hackneyed phrases get old and meaningless very fast. You are probably using them too much.

At the end of the day, I wish it were the end of the day.

What's the Plan?

There is that nagging question that comes up every day, "What's the PLAN?" It conjures up guilt and questions about self-worth. Plans come by many names—it could be called the strategy, it could be the plain old budget, or it could be called something exotic like "the Five Pillars to Success." My favorite name is the ROAD MAP.

The world demands it. Your boss requires it. Your spouse wonders about it. You need a plan.

Those of you who take public transit to work are lucky. You are not clicking through the radio trying to understand where the traffic problems are every day. The rest of us probably spend too much time in the car, which raises the question, how do we use that time?

FM radio is okay but I am sick of most of the songs since I am stuck in my car listening to FM radio. Texting is never an option. Talk radio can be okay, but it seems too loud and shrill for the morning.

Here is an idea: on the way to work, while in your car, plan your day. On the way home from work, reflect on the day. Each day, use that commute time a little more productively. It might help you be more effective and get a raise. And then, you can get a better car for commuting.

There will be lots of meetings in December where we plot out the plan for the new year. There will be flip charts and markers and yellow stickies and breakout groups and facilitators in conference rooms and hotels all over the country.

And the first topic of conversation over coffee and muffins will be, "Do we need a mission statement?"

The response will be, "No, I think we need a vision."

And the third comment will be the question, "What is the difference between a vision and a mission?"

That discussion will go until lunchtime with no clear resolution. Aaaargh.

The three things we all want to know at work are: what's my job, how am I doing, and how does my effort make us more successful?

A little time on those questions might be more productive than a framed vision statement on the wall.

A road map *should* tell you how to get to where you want to go and the stops along the way. The corporate road map, of course, assumes you know where you are going, which is not always the case.

The problem with so many corporate road maps is that they are too complicated so no one pays any attention to them.

I think there is a lot to be learned from my favorite road map—the kids' game Chutes and Ladders. Just like work, the game is all about rewards and consequences. With good deeds you climb, and for misbehavior you go down chutes. Plus, in the game you know where you are and you can see the end.

Need a good road map? Just look in the toy bin, then implement it.

Does Low-Hanging Fruit Exist?

"First, we will go after the low-hanging fruit." We have all heard that comment and it makes my hair catch on fire. It is a big mistake. Do not go there. Looking for that fruit is a false hope.

Low-hanging fruit does not exist. If it ever existed, it was picked long ago. The mention of low-hanging fruit conjures up images of apples hanging down at eye level screaming, "Pick me, pick me!" The expectation that there are easy ways to make things change leads to disappointment when we run through the proverbial orchard and find no fruit.

Going after low-hanging fruit implies which things we should do first. That is, pick the fruit that is easiest to reach. Bad approach. Most often, the first things that must be done are the most difficult.

Ask any fruit picker about low-hanging fruit. The picker will point out that the fruit at the top of the tree is ripe first and more plentiful. The return for the effort is at the top of the tree.

Selecting easy targets that require no effort reflects what we all want the world to be like. Picking a few low-hanging things may get things started but won't amount to much. Unless you live in an orchard, your encounters with low-hanging fruit won't actually come very often.

Low-hanging fruit may be appealing and easy, but it may not be the right thing to talk about or pursue. Ask Adam how it worked out for him with that low-hanging apple.

The Chickens Need a Raise

Certain jobs make me say to myself, "However much that person is being paid, it is not enough."

When I sit in my office on the twenty-third floor and I see the guy outside my window washing it, it's a no-brainer that I think he should get a raise. Coal miners deserve a raise, as do deep-water divers and every law enforcement person in the world, no matter how much money they make. The dangerous jobs are always ones that make me wonder about the risk–reward ratio.

A new group of workers makes me scratch my head about the pay versus job satisfaction equation. These are the people who dress like a chicken to get us into the restaurant. Or dress as Bullwinkle the moose to get us to visit the time-share office. Or dress as the Statue of Liberty to get us into the car wash.

I suspect it's the minimum wage for these brave souls who need to be energetic too. I think they deserve a raise.

Showing Up Still Matters

Working hard and showing up are not the same thing. Both things are important. Even in a world that can look like a cube farm and where everyone is looking at computers all day and wearing headphones, engagement and relationships matter.

When a friend was fired, he was shocked. WTF! He was yelling at everyone. His employer said he was let go because of his poor attendance record. Attendance record? Really? Is this high school?! He knew he worked like a dog and never heard anything about attendance. Who takes attendance?

Maybe it was not just about attendance. Between traveling and working from home at all hours, the guy thought he was meeting all of his objectives. So what happened?

No one knew him. Being around the place still matters. Hanging around with the boss still matters. Being a colleague still matters. Being part of the team still matters, even in a virtual world. It's easier to get rid of people no one knows.

Show up. Have coffees with colleagues. Go to the holiday party. The thing is, someone *is* taking attendance.

The Working from Home Thing

The notion of working from home is a powerful one. We all want to do it. I want to do it. I want to avoid that commute and get away from all those distractions in the office. At home, no one is asking, "Do you have a minute?" That "minute" ends up taking an hour.

When I work from home I get all settled in for grinding it out. I am Mr. Productivity. Then the doorbell rings and it is either the UPS guy or an Amazon delivery. Wonder what that could be. Then the dog needs to go out for a long walk. Hey, there is that magazine I've been looking for. And what's for lunch?

During the conference call the dog starts barking and the others on the call start asking questions. "What's that noise?" "Is there a dog on the call?" I chime in, "Whoever is with that dog, please put your phone on mute."

Then it's time to deal with the tech equipment because all of a sudden there is no Internet connection and I need to get that presentation out and there is no one to help. I am on hold with tech support.

Now it's time to pick up the kids at school. Having them at home will help me focus.

Working at home can be a real boon to productivity.

Are You Responsive?

My first boss told me in no uncertain terms: THESE ARE THE RULES, and they should never be broken if you want to be successful.

- Every phone call should be returned within twenty-four hours. Even those from people you don't know.
- Every memo should have a response by the next business day. Even if the response is, "I am in receipt of your memo, stay tuned."
- Each piece of correspondence received should be acknowledged and a response prepared and returned within three business days.

Today, it is rare to make a phone call or to receive one. No one even knows what a memo is anymore, and no one receives written letters unless the letter is from the IRS. The rules have changed and are now, well, a little ambiguous. There are some general guidelines, like:

- An e-mail needs to be returned the same day. Probably.
- A text should be returned in five minutes. Probably.
- And a phone call? Depending on who it is, maybe someone will get around to it eventually.

Some would say that these guideline response times are too slow. This group would say an e-mail should be returned within the hour and a text within a minute. This same group would be forgiving on returned phone call times because this is the group that never makes phone calls or would die before posting an automatic out-of-office response.

Others would say e-mails, texts, and calls are the source of all distractions and inefficiencies. This group would choose not to be measured by response time.

The workplace is moving so fast today that "the quicker the response, the better" is always a good rule. Acceptable and exact response times today are a moving target with lots of variables that dictate the right answer.

One thing I do know: to be labeled as unresponsive in today's workplace is the kiss of laziness and a step toward the exit door.

Coffee Is the New Lunch and Other Coffee Matters

Lunch is dead. It takes too long, it's too crowded, and it's a hassle. Besides, it is often offered for free or at a big discount if you stay in the company cafeteria. So instead of lunch out at the local restaurant where one can network and maybe even interview for new jobs, we are stuck with our colleagues who complain about the boss. The solution is coffee, whether you drink it or not.

Coffee is no longer an innocent drink to have with the morning doughnut in private. Coffee isn't even a drink. Coffee may not even involve coffee. When someone asks you out for a coffee, it means a short meeting outside of the office. It could be purely social (even a date), it could be all about business, it could be just good networking, or, most likely, it could be an interview. Most importantly, "coffee" means not too long.

There are many benefits to "coffee," including:

- It's possible to have five coffees or more in a day. You can only have one lunch.
- Lunch can be lots of calories. Coffee is nonfattening unless you order a huge Mocha Frappuccino with extra caramel.
- Coffee frees up lunch to get real work done. You can still have that turkey sandwich at your desk at lunch, knowing that you already had five coffees.

In our drive for efficiency and productivity, lunch is being replaced with coffee. Lunch is now reserved for true friends and making deals. It is a special event.

The place for the two activities is reversed. Lunch is probably now in the office and coffee is outside of the office. A typical coffee shop is more like a career fair, with interviews taking place at every non-private little table. I see people discussing their strengths and weaknesses everywhere while their coffee gets cold. So I tried conducting an interview in the local beanery, thinking that it would put the candidate more at ease. The alternative was a stark conference room, which does not lend itself to participants feeling at ease. In the coffee shop, as always, there was a line while the barista did her thing, so we broke the ice over small talk. When it came our time to order, my candidate ordered a Mocha Coconut Frappuccino, blended, with foam on the side. Extra hot.

"Is this a person who is going to be high maintenance?" I wondered. If ordering a coffee is this complicated, how will this person do when it comes to putting a plan together? Is it right to judge people by the coffee they order? Right or wrong, when looking for a job, we are all judged by every small movement. Could be our clothes or hairstyle or where we went to school—or our coffee order.

When I entertained yet another candidate for a job, I learned about coffee names by chance. My candidate, who was named Joaquim, was asked his name. He replied, "Joe." It turns out, about half of us have coffee names, and that's a good thing. Coffee names are all about clarity and ease of completion. No need to spell Ann, Joe, or Scott. Coffee names are all about efficiency, and short names make the line go faster. Coffee names are all about creativity too. What name can we dream up that captures our essence without having to spell it every time? Coffee names can create an alter ego too. If we can change our name at the coffee corner, the superhero in the office can't be far behind.

Coffee is an important part of the workplace that can make or break a career all at once. Coffee is more than a caffeine buzz; it is a parallel universe to the office. Remember what can happen over coffee and save the mocha frappés for when you get a job.

What Is That Smell?

The advent of microwave ovens created a brave new world at work. The office no longer needed to reek of printer toner and whiteboard markers alone. The office could now smell of microwave popcorn!

Ah, but it didn't stop there. We can pop something out of the freezer (with the notes on it about cleaning up after yourself) and cook a lasagna or chicken potpie. Going even further, the microwave is now the new home for cooking leftovers. How many of us have been distracted by what we know is a reheated bean burrito or beef chow mein that was nuked just a little too long? The smell of reheated burritos can be as distracting as the guy in the cubicle next door who talks to his mother all day.

I dare you to hold a serious meeting when the smell from the garlic in the clam linguini works its way through the halls. The mind wanders in the hope that we don't sit next to that person in the next meeting. What was not eaten at the restaurant last night does not go home, it ends up in the office microwave. The odors are shared by all.

Some say that leftovers in the office create community when everyone goes out in the hall and asks, what is that smell? Who is cooking that? Leftovers allow colleagues to share their restaurant experiences, and leftovers are the inspiration for the ironclad rule about implementation: whatever is left in the refrigerator on Friday will be thrown away.

It is always good to know that inspiration about execution can come from new sources, like leftovers. And sometimes they are best left at home.

Making a To-Do List Is Not the Same As Getting Something Done

It's a trap. The trap is a false sense of activity. You think you're busy, and, in fact, you may be really busy, but is anything that matters really getting done? Are you advancing the cause or just filling up the calendar? Take a look at the calendar—how much of the activity really matters?

There are clear symptoms if you suffer from the "false sense of activity" syndrome. Symptom one is feeling like you are in too many meetings. By definition, too many meetings means you are busy but getting nothing done. Symptom one leads to symptom two, which is that you are always late. Another killer symptom is reviewing your to-do list and finding that the only things that ever come off are the easy things. The big, tough things to do are always left for another day. When you leave the workplace at the end of they day, if you ever ask yourself, "What did I really do today?" you are suffering from a false sense of activity. It can become a nasty habit and your colleagues believe you are busy but you really are not.

Some big things can move a mile a year. Some things only move an inch a year. Just move something.

Can We Cancel All Meetings but Keep the Doughnuts?

When my son was three years old he would occasionally call for a meeting. He didn't know what a meeting was but he heard all the adults talking about meetings so he thought they must be something worth exploring. We dissuaded him of the notion.

Some companies are eliminating the performance review process. Why not keep going and eliminate meetings? We like the doughnuts, we don't like the smell of dry erase markers and questions like, "Can we do a process check?"

Would the world end if we eliminated meetings? What would happen if we just stopped meeting?

- Communication would suffer. Or would it? Between e-mail, texting, and checking out all the posts on social media, would we communicate less?
- Colleagues would not work together as well. Maybe. It does help to know one another, but is partnering enhanced through meetings?
- Coordination between teams would be limited, we might duplicate each other's activities, and calendars would be a big mess. The alternative could be checking project schedules and checking for intersections. Maybe the projects would get completed earlier.
- Team building would not exist. I am not sure most people look at meetings as team-building activities. Lunch is more likely to be seen as team-building time. At a time when lots of people work at home, team building can come when time spent together outside of meetings is scheduled.

The alternatives to meetings now include conference calls and actual one-to-one phone calls with people talking. Plus, the daily "coffee" with pals and lunch are now requirements. Things do get resolved in these interactions. People figure out how to get together to solve problems without having a routine meeting.

Think of the money that could be saved—whiteboard markers would never dry up. Conference rooms could be rented out for Airbnb use. Think of the weight we could lose by not sitting for hours and eating doughnuts. Wait, keep the doughnuts, just put them in the kitchen.

Meetings are habit forming. We are trained in how to conduct effective meetings, but maybe we should be trained in whether or not we really need to have the meeting.

Big, progressive companies have eliminated the routine performance review. Why not move on to meetings. Can we try it? Should we have a meeting about it?

How Late Is Late?

The text flashed while I was sitting at the coffee shop. "I'm running a little late," my coffee date said. She was already five minutes late, so that was not a surprise. "No worries," I texted back. "How late will you be?" The text reply was "@45 minutes."

Argh, that is really, really late. Late enough that if I waited, my day would be totally disrupted. So we rescheduled for several weeks out. And it was her loss because she was the one who wanted the meeting.

Each of us has dealt with the late person. Sure, it's annoying, since no one wants to be left at the altar or the blueberry muffin counter. At the moment you realize your business "date" will be late you have two choices.

1. You can let it ruin your day. You can be out of sorts, kick your metaphorical dog, and be mean to the person who is late, regardless of the excuse.
2. You can sigh and use the time productively. Enjoy the latte you bought, check out the news, and catch up on those e-mails you need to get to.

I recommend option two.

Most of us don't plan to be late and don't enjoy being late, but it happens. And when it does, the real question becomes, how late is late? Let's start with this: being late is never a good thing. Almost always, for the one who is tardy there is stress, a bursting bladder, and a dead cell phone. Being late is never fun for the offender.

In a day when business casual could mean shorts and flip-flops and when dogs hang around at the office, what does late mean? It means not on time. (According to some, not being fifteen minutes early is late.) Five minutes late is within a reasonable range and worthy of the good-effort grade. Fifteen minutes late is pushing it on the forgiveness scale. And anything after that is just rude and requires making a big apology and picking up the check. Thirty minutes late will have you wondering why you scheduled the meeting in the first place because it will probably not start out well.

Excuses and reasons why one is late sort of don't matter. You are still late. Traffic is no longer a good excuse because there is always traffic. You need to bake that into plans and schedules. Good excuses do exist and usually involve blood or children.

Late means the same thing on both ends of the business equation, whether it is a lunch date or a job interview. A late interviewer is just as rude as a late job candidate. A late customer is just as rude as a late sales rep.

For the latecomers, here are some traps to avoid:

- Don't overbook yourself. It will guarantee that you are always behind schedule and always late.
- Don't be known as the one who is always late. It will brand you in a disorganized and not happy way.
- Don't assume that travel will ever go as planned. It never does and you need to bake in lots of time for problems.
- Don't arrange a meeting without the cell number of the person you are meeting. If there is a big issue you can contact your date.

Unlike many other rules in business that are morphing and changing, the late rule has not changed. Late is late.

To paraphrase Shakespeare, "better an hour too soon than a minute too late."

The IT Guy Is the Most Important Person You Know

The IT guy can be a man or woman, young or old, and any race or ethnicity imaginable. The IT guy can be in the cubicle next to you or ten thousand miles away. In any and all cases, the IT guy is someone to cherish. The IT guy alone is a reason to keep your job.

Being employed puts you in the "have" category. As in, "I have a job." Looking for employment puts you in the "have not" category, whether you are an investment banker or a custodian. Economists, psychologists, and parents all have opinions about why it is important to a person's well-being that he or she hold a steady job. The reasons range from cash flow to having a reason to get up in the morning.

When it comes to work and why we do it, the research all points to things like we derive a sense of worth or we want to make an impact or we derive satisfaction from helping others. The paycheck is a good reason to work too. Those are all good things, but on a day-to-day basis, my research shows there are two big reasons that people work.

The first reason is to keep health-care benefits in place. Trying to figure out benefit options, no less pay for them, is overwhelming. Some say it is worth keeping even a not-so-good job just for the benefits. With health-care legislation constantly changing, it is growing more difficult to figure out. With a traditional job, the worries about benefits are much less.

The second reason to keep a job is to have a relationship with the IT guy. Yes, that guy. With a job, you don't need to depend on your fifteen-year-old neighbor. You have that guy, and your frozen laptop can be fixed without you feeling guilty or going to the computer store. The IT guy can link your devices without causing a meltdown and retrieve data that you thought was lost. The IT guy is the one you can count on to fix your ever more technical life. And the IT guy gets paid to help you—that's the job.

So next time you feel sorry for yourself while you are stuck in traffic on the way to work, just say to yourself, "At least I have benefits and the IT guy." You will feel better and be on the road to getting something done.

Dogs in the Halls

Let me first say I love dogs. My family has always had dogs. We have two dogs right now and one of them is the smartest person in our family. Now that's out of the way, and I can say what I think about dogs at work.

Keep the dogs home. Or at least don't bring them to work.

Spending time at some of the tech start-up companies is like visiting a kennel. The dogs run around among the work spaces having a great old time. The little dogs chase the big ones and they all sniff each other's butts and snarf around for bagels on the floor. Hygiene problems are abundant as the dogs avail themselves of any open space to make their mark.

The dogs bark at the UPS guy, jump up on candidates who show up for interviews, beg for food and attention, and distract all who are trying to concentrate. Some dogs are small enough to fit in a purse, and they stay there for fear they could be eaten by the bigger dogs.

Other than that, there are no problems with having dogs around.

Call me old-fashioned, but unless you live on a sheep farm or are working in your garage with one other person, I am not sure dogs belong at work.

That Double-Secret Probation Thing

Probation is a word we don't hear much anymore when it comes to work. Maybe there is too much of a "just out of prison" connotation for us to feel comfortable with the word.

Too bad, because although the word seems to have fallen out of use, the concept is very much still in place. Especially when we begin a job, our every move is being watched to see if we fit. When we are on probation, every e-mail is important, what we say in any meeting is critical, and how we will work with the team is even more examined.

And it works both ways; probation is a time when we can see whether or not we really want to be a part of this new thing. Probationary periods really do matter.

The truth is, no matter what we call it, we are all on probation every day at work. Don't forget.

All My Mentors Are Dead

Everybody wants one. Some places mandate that you have one. They say a good one will guarantee success. Finding one and being one can be tricky.

Mentors are a hot topic. But finding a mentor and working with one can be a little complicated. It would seem an easy enough transaction. During our careers, especially early on, we need guidance and counsel about how to be effective and how to navigate through complex organizations. Who better to do that than a mentor? Someone who has been there, done that. We need someone who can be inspirational and all knowing at the same time. Think Obi-Wan Kenobi, Yoda, and Mr. Miyagi in the cubicle next to yours and always available.

Forget Obi-Wan. The cubicle next door is more likely to house a stream of people wearing headphones who don't know you exist. And the truth is, Yoda or Mr. Miyagi rarely exist at work. So the mentor dance begins.

The mentee can't take the lead in the dance; there are just too many questions. Like the first dance with a partner, questions from mentee to mentor are awkward. What dance will we do? What if there is no chemistry? Will it be a coaching relationship? (You can finish this project!) Will it be a counselor kind of thing? (How do you feel about that?) Will it be a directive relationship? (Okay, do this, then this...) The questions can make us shy about seeking a mentor.

The mentor has a lot of questions too. Do I have the time to do this right? (Probably not.) Does anyone really care? (Probably not.) Is this like an extracurricular activity? (Probably so.) I don't have a mentor, why should I be one? (HR says so.) What if I don't like my mentee, can I opt out or trade for a different one? Everyone is too busy and the questions can make us reticent to serve as a mentor.

So many questions, so many mentees, so few mentors.

Everyone tells us we need one. We all want one but it's hard to find one. It's to the point where both mentors and mentees can feel a little guilty if they are not part of the "dance." Experts tell all of us that we should be mentors and if you don't have a mentee, find one. More guilt.

My solution? Until you find the ideal mentor or mentee, pick a virtual mentor, depending on the situation.

For example, when faced with a desperate situation, ask yourself, "What would Abraham Lincoln do?"

Or, "How would Meryl Streep react to so much attention?" They may never know it, but lots of people dead and alive are acting like mentors every day. And at a time when mentors are hard to find, it might be the best you can do. And virtual mentors can be good dance partners.

I have been lucky along the way to have very good live mentors. Each of them knew me well, spent time with me, and did not hesitate to give positive and negative feedback.

Good luck hunting and dancing with real and imagined mentors.

The Three Best Business Books Ever Written

Anyone who writes business books is asked the same question: "What is your favorite business book?" (Other than the one you have written.) It seems that literally hundreds of business books are written each week, so it is increasingly hard to discern the good ones from the bad ones. Some are CEO vanity books, some are two ideas that stretch out to three hundred pages. Since I do write business books and I am asked that question about the best ones, I surprise people with my answer. To me, the three best business books are not specific to authors. They are not specific to a discipline. They are not specific to a particular school of thought or methodology.

I would wager that if I did a survey of most executives regarding the three best books, they would be able to easily name them, including the author and maybe even when the books were published. Regardless of the titles and times, I would wager also that the executives could place the books into one of three categories. And it is those three categories that make the books we remember and refer to. There is no magic but neither is there empirical evidence. My idea of the three best business books ever written is not what you might expect, but here it is:

1. **The book that saved your career.** You know the one; you needed an answer quickly for the boss or the board or the Wall Street analyst and there was that one book that had just the right answer at just the right time. The book may have included the ratio you needed or the diagram you needed—no modification required. The book made you look good.

2. **The book that is a constant reference.** This is the book that may have lots of dog-eared pages from constant use. It reminds you of the difference between a Gantt chart and a Venn diagram and Harvey Balls. It's the book that shows you once again how to create a cap table or what Black and Scholes came up with a while back. This book might tell you how to do a tough performance review. And you know right where to look in this book for help.

3. **The book that provides comfort.** It's the book that tells you that you are doing the right thing. This is the book that might include chapters on ethics and how to be a good boss. It might be a book with advice about changing careers or work–life balance. Probably the book will tell you that success in business is as much art as it is science. It is the book that you glance at near the end of the day for reassurance.

You know the good business book by the one that is your friend versus the one you buy and never open. Business books don't need to be complicated, just helpful. Like this one.

The Thing About Getting Hired and Fired

It is a mystery, that thing about job hunting. In the same news report I heard that there are five million job openings and that there are five million unemployed. It sounds easy to just do a little matching but it is not that easy. Hired and fired—both are times of disappointment, rejection, silence, and, in some special cases, elation.

Getting hired is barely more of a rational path than getting fired. It can involve timing, connections, and directions from the Magic 8 Ball. Even in our era of sophisticated modeling and analytics, even with resume scanners and job search scrapers, even with millions of pieces written about how to find that next exciting job, to nearly everyone looking for that new position, how to find one is a mystery.

Sometimes people get hired because they are available.

Sometimes people get hired just so they will stop bugging the people in HR.

Sometimes people get hired because a relative is the boss.

Sometimes people get hired because they showed up.

Sometimes people get hired because they are qualified, competent, and can really do the job.

Sometimes there are no jobs and people just don't get hired.

The irony is that hiring and firing are probably the two processes that are the most well documented and prescribed in all organizations. Hundreds of books have been written about both job hunting and rebounding after a setback like being terminated. Despite all the documentation and advice, everyone has unhappy stories about the entire mess. Some solutions are offered among these essays. More likely, I will provide a few insights that will help you cope. Work is a good thing, and the process of getting and keeping a meaningful position is critical to our emotional and financial well-being. Frustrating as it can be, treat getting hired and rebounding from getting sacked with all with the zeal they deserve. Success will follow. I am sure of it.

Getting Hired Is a Probability Function

Someone asked me recently how I would describe the job hunt process. I could tell that the person asking the question wanted me to say that it was the most onerous thing in the world, that it is depressing, full of rejection and disappointment, and that it is something to dread.

My response was a simple metaphor: job hunting is like fishing. Without bait in the water you won't catch any fish. And the more bait, the more fish catching is possible. And you need to have the right fishing gear and be prepared for what the fish are biting on.

The thing is, like fishing, job hunting requires lots of patience, and some days you don't catch any fish. Most days you might not catch any fish and you need to be prepared for that.

What you do with the fish once you catch them is up to you. I recommend you make the most of any fish you catch. Even the small fish may tide you over until the big one jumps in the boat. And fish where the fish are.

Networking—It's All About Traffic

Traffic. You probably sit in it much more than you want to and you hate it. The talk radio shows and classic rock stations get old. The bane of most lives is the morning and afternoon commute. We do the commute to be close to relatives, for better schools, or for a more affordable house, and we try to use the time effectively but there are only so many things to do while stuck in traffic. Traffic with a capital T is now what the workplace is all about.

The workplace used to be about being stuck *in* traffic. Now, it's about driving traffic and being out in traffic.

Driving traffic is a measure of your competency and a measure of your "platform." Your platform is what you have created about yourself, your brand, based on the traffic you generate on social media. The more traffic, the bigger the platform, and the more employers notice you might be an expert in something or have something to say besides what happened in college. The ability to drive traffic can lead to that job you want.

Or, being "out in traffic" can lead to that job you want. That is, never miss a chance to network, to have lunch, to buy a coffee, to build a new relationship, so that people know you are competent and cool.

One guy I know frequented the deli downstairs and every day ordered a turkey sandwich on wheat. He then went back to his cubicle and continued to work, all the time thinking he would get ahead by not wasting time on lunch. The guy in the cubicle next to the turkey sandwich guy went out to lunch every day and was promoted faster. You have to be out in traffic, and the opportunities for creating traffic are limitless. You can be in the swirl of traffic on social media, over coffee, at the gym, or at a lunch out of the office.

Traffic doesn't come to you; it takes some effort to get out there, and the merge into it in the beginning may not be easy. In the workplace today, if you are not out in traffic, you are being left behind.

Words That Matter in the Hunt

Half the people I know are looking for a new job. The other half are worried about their job. The third half like their jobs but are "open" to new opportunities. In this world where everyone is sort of career trolling, words matter. My friends go to job-search sites and have lots of meetings at the local coffee pub discussing words that will help their careers, like "maximized" and "strategized." They spend hours fretting over the words they hear from employers and the words that will best capture their experience and hopes and dreams. It's not easy to be so worried about words.

They wait for responses from anyone out there—employers, networking opportunities, invitations to meetups, anything! It is a cruel waiting game. Having been caught in that waiting game from time to time myself, I believe there are only two words that matter.

One short but critical word that matters is "PLEASED." As in, Ms. Smith, we are pleased to invite you in for an interview or, better yet, we are pleased to offer you this great job.

The only other word that matters is "UNFORTUNATELY." No matter what is said before or after that word, it means rejection. As in, Mr. Jones, you are the best thing to come along since cheese graters, unfortunately... you know how it continues.

If employers wanted to be really efficient, they could just send out e-mails with a heading of "unfortunately" or "pleased." It might move things along quickly and would be better than never hearing anything at all. Here's hoping that you receive more "pleased" than "unfortunately" words.

Gigs Are a Beautiful Thing

Listen to the employment prospects of any rock and roll band and you will hear them talking about the next gig. As in, our next gig is in Cleveland, or we are just happy to have another gig. Gig is a good word, and although the actual word may not make any sense, everyone knows what it means when it comes to a rock band. There is a certain breeziness to it that connotes being young and careless—although you may not know where the next gig is coming from, who cares, things always work out.

The same term should be part of your job hunt vernacular, because many say we are in a "gig economy." For those of us not in a rock band it means you may not know where your next project is coming from and you have no health-care benefits, but it is better than staying home and watching daytime TV. And if you do really well on any gig, who knows, you may just get discovered.

A gig may not mean you are carefree and happy playing music, but the thing is, it may mean a paycheck until a more permanent job comes along.

Tell Me About Yourself and Other Lies

We have all been in job interviews when the interviewer utters those dreaded words: tell me about yourself. It is not a question, and I always suspect the interviewer really doesn't want to know, but it is the most legally safe way to start a conversation.

The response I always *want* to give is, what do you want to know? Where I was born? Where I went to college? Did my mother beat me? That I need to lose weight? That I am desperate for this job? Gimme a hint. Please.

Instead, we all play along because we sort of know that the interviewer is really asking what I have done that is important to this job and how I think it will help them. It's the game we all sign up for when looking for a job. If it's a sales job, we mention those sales records for Girl Scout cookies. If it's a writing job we highlight that we are descended from James Joyce.

The other dreaded interview question is, do you have any questions? What I really want to ask is, how much vacation do I get? Or, when is my first raise? Or, is it true there is free food every day? Instead, we all ask questions like, are there opportunities for growth?

The thing is, if we all asked what we really wanted to know and answered questions with 100 percent honesty, the job search process would be way more efficient. In the meantime, do your best to get the job when playing the Q&A game. More truth can come out later.

Coffee Can Kill a Career

Job interviews in stark cubicles or conference rooms are dead. A job interview now is more likely to be conducted at the local coffee stand. While the barista is grinding out today's fresh roast, you may be asked about your strengths and weaknesses.

Don't be fooled, an interview in a Starbucks is no less an evaluation than one held in the conference room on the fortieth floor. In a virtual world, the coffee shop might be the *only* place to do the interview, since neither of you has an office.

As I have watched the "coffee interview" unfold, one easy-to-follow guideline applies: order something simple. What you order says something about you as much as your clothes. I saw a candidate who was dressed for success, and after waiting in line with a charming repartee, order a...tall iced coffee in a Grande cup with extra ice, three pumps hazelnut, with a dome lid and a Venti straw. She didn't get the job. Anyone who is that much work over coffee will be no fun to work with in a planning session.

An interview (or deal making) over coffee is not a casual affair. Those around you may be reading the newspaper but you might be at the most important meeting of your year. Don't let your guard down, and just order a small latte.

Why Do Interviewers Talk So Much?

You are the one being interviewed but the interviewer is too busy talking to ask any questions. How will he ever get to know you? Is it already too late to get the job? Are you being dismissed? Are you supposed to care about the interviewer's golf scores? You want to say, "Shut up! It's too bad your kids are sick but I need you to listen to me!"

What if your time is up and you hardly had a chance to talk? Does that mean you are so good that they don't need to know any more about you? Probably not. So how do you turn the conversation back to the most important person in the interview, you?

It is time for an intervention. Once you feel the time is slipping away, as well as your chances, interrupt. You will soon have nothing to lose. Don't panic in the first five minutes but if you are halfway through the interview and you still haven't had time to talk, it is time for the interruption. No need to be rude, but interrupt.

Politely say, "Thanks for all that information, fascinating, can I tell you now how my experience relates to this job?" And then don't stop talking. You can save the day, or not, but at least you left an impression.

Hello? Anyone Out There?

It doesn't matter. The economy can be robust or it can be in the sewer. The jobs can be in tech or energy, or there may be none available. Regardless, there are always millions of people looking for a job. It is an ongoing and constant phenomenon; there are no surprises.

So why is it, then, that as people seek fame and fortune, one huge frustration emerges—applicants never hear back from places they have applied. Not a word. After spending hours filling out forms from employers (they are never the same), no courtesy, no response, just silence.

Employers, you can do better. You have technologies that can scrape resumes for key words like brand names and college degrees. You have sophisticated CRM systems, you have cloud computing and big data available. Employers, you know that no reply to someone who pours her soul into an application is a little rude. You wouldn't like it. The least you can do is respond with a note that says, "Thanks for applying. Stay tuned."

Or better yet, how about a response that says, "Thanks for applying. We can see you are a talented man/woman. Come on in to discuss your interests further. We can't wait to see you."

The response may not be practical but it would lead to a happier world.

Reference Checking and Your Secrets

In a reference check it is illegal for employers to give out more information than the dates of employment. That's it. All any employer can say is, "Jane Doe was employed here between these dates..." Then why are reference checks so important? Because people find out EVERYTHING about you when doing those checks.

The HR department divulges only dates of employment but everyone else blabs like crazy. Some references treat such calls as a way to help you. Others see a call as a way to get even with you. Most are either oblivious to employment laws or ignore them. In reference calls I have conducted I have learned about dating history, religious beliefs, attendance records, and quirky personality traits. Then the reference might get into all the bad things that I really don't want to know. Like the time there was a drunken incident at the holiday party and a reference to YouTube videos.

The lessons are simple. First, be very careful who you list as a reference. There will be probing questions. Second, be prepared to address any issues that may come to light. Third, don't do anything that will reflect poorly on you in the future.

Act every day like what you do will show up on YouTube and, eventually, in a reference check.

The Interns Are Coming

It is now practically a requirement for college students everywhere: an internship. Interns are everywhere. I can spot them because they are always looking around trying to figure out what they really should be doing.

Based on what I see, there are two kinds of interns. There are those who will do anything to build a resume and pay is no issue. Key words like Uganda, orphanage, and not-for-profit pop up around these interns, and the experience could be truly life changing. Many photos are associated with these internships.

The other kind of intern is one who wants money and knows that certain internships pay well because, often, no one really wants to do this work. Key words here are sewer, tree removal, and picking fruit. These internships used to be called summer jobs but now one learns leadership and organizational skills while breaking concrete sidewalks for the department of public works.

Okay, there are three kinds of interns. The last type of intern manages to find something that pays well *and* looks good on the resume. These are the toughest to find, and good luck. Key words here are Google, hen's teeth, and perfect SAT scores. These interns are often computer science people who went to the right school and may or may not be very popular.

The old summer job standbys like camp counselor, lifeguard, and waitress are still available and shouldn't be dismissed, even though the word intern is not associated with them. The experience can be just as meaningful, but it takes a little more work to describe the work in a way that will relate to a real job. Key words here are: work hard, have fun, and make friends.

Unless you work at Electronic Arts or a company that develops games, sitting around playing video games for weeks at a time is not an internship. Key words are waste of time and talent.

If you are managing an intern, be gentle. If you are an intern, be a sponge.

Performance Review Benedictions

When annual performance review time is over, everyone is thankful to whatever God they worship. For some, the review was a happy day. For others, not so much. For most, it is somewhere in the middle. Most of us are just glad to have the process over with so we can move on. And that is exactly the lesson to be learned from the annual review process—move on.

In your organization some get promoted and others don't. You should celebrate or despair for a day, but then you move on. Some make more money, some less; some get to sit at the grown-up table, some in the peanut gallery; some get to have a big birthday party at work; some were born on holidays and miss having birthday parties. Still, move on.

Sometimes emotions need to be set aside and replaced with resolve. Big things need to be accomplished, the paycheck still needs to get deposited, and your career needs to be built. Perspective is required.

Zig Ziglar, the great sales motivator, coached everyone to be optimistic, to be generous, and to always keep things in perspective. He told the story of the woman who hated her job and her coworkers. She just HATED everything. He suggested to her that she wake up each day, stare in the mirror, and say how much she loved her job. When he bumped into her later she told him she was doing much better because all the people she worked with had really changed.

Never get wrapped up in cudda, wudda, shoulda. Those who seem to be the most successful and happy at work are the ones who know how to move on. Join that club.

Get Fired at Least Once—It Can Be Good for Your Career

The last time I was fired was during a training exercise for everyone except me. That is, an "up-and-comer" needed to learn how to properly terminate someone. I was that someone. It had been planned for weeks, maybe months, and "they" (you know who the proverbial "they" can be) wanted to use it as a means to "season" a young principal in the firm. So "they" all showed up. "Them" on one side of the conference table, me on the other side. The corporate attorney, who I thought was my friend, sitting on the opposite side of the table didn't inspire confidence in my chances.

"We are going to discontinue your service here," was the salvo the young buck used as an opener. I wanted to ask, "What the f##k does that mean?" but I was silent. I now knew what was happening and I didn't want to play my hand in case there was a juicy severance to negotiate.

The job wasn't that important to me. In fact, I didn't like it that much and was thinking about quitting anyway, but now I was really pissed. I wanted to be anywhere except in that room with the little guy who was anointed to do the dirty deed. He could have sent me an e-mail with the word "unfortunately" as the header. Or, if he wanted to be verbose, he could have proclaimed, "Due to business circumstances beyond our control..." I could have taken it from there.

No one had said anything during the entire time except for my executioner. He had typed out notes and he was reading through the litany of all my shortcomings over the last few years while I was wondering what to do with the Lucite cubes in my now unnecessary office. Some of the observers looked at me intently to see if I would start crying, others looked down as if they were praying. Turns out, my misdemeanors ranged from assigning low-level work to low-level people to missing the company picnic to not doing enough math homework in high school. A few others were mentioned, probably more substantive, but I don't remember them.

It all took waaay longer than it should have taken and I was not given a chance to talk or rebut about the time I left the dirty dishes in the sink or took the last cup of coffee and didn't make a new pot. It didn't matter at that point. And even though I knew it didn't matter, I started sorting out in my mind all the good things I had done for which I was now receiving no credit.

What about that time I flew all night for a half-baked meeting?

What about the time I helped your stupid former wife get a job?

What about the time I made us all that money?

None of it mattered and I mentioned none of it. At this point it was all flotsam and jetsam of an old job.

At the conclusion, while I was sitting there after having just been dumped, the senior guy in the room turned to the trainee who had just fired me and proudly boomed, "Nicely done!"

Nicely done? Are you kidding me? It was not nicely done. It was a travesty and I was the victim. I wanted to reach across the table and wring his neck. If he had been wearing a tie I would have twisted it around his neck. He was not wearing a tie and I did nothing. That's what pretty much everyone does, nothing. Maybe a document is signed that promises not to sue or maybe some vacation time is negotiated, but the old gang of "they" is running the controls in any meeting where someone loses a job.

My feelings were hurt. That was that, I was out. In a matter of seconds, everything I was working on mattered not at all. In a matter of a short meeting that could have been shorter, my relationship with the entire place had changed—no one would look at me and I pretty much hated them all.

No verbs like axed, booted, canned, sacked, kicked out, given marching orders, pink slipped, laid off, let go, ousted, sacked, or terminated were ever even used. My services were discontinued.

I moved on and lived for another job. But it took a minute for me to not think of creating voodoo dolls of my former "close" colleagues and filling the eyes of the dolls with poison pins.

And yet, it happens every day, probably millions of times. Someone is getting fired and someone else is doing the firing. Every Friday afternoon someone will say, "Hey, Cindy, meet me in the conference room at four, I have something important to discuss."

Or, "Hey, Bob, bring your company ID badge with you when we meet later." Cindy and Bob show up and they are read their last rights from an HR rep about COBRA, where to turn in the company computer, and why they can no longer attend the company beer bash on Friday. Then they go to the bar around the corner with their now former coworkers and agree on what assholes manage the old place.

Being fired can be good for your career. It will definitely bring humility into your life. As the song says, no one is irreplaceable. And your sudden change in job status can bring some perspective about that job that you thought defined you. It can provide an opportunity to take stock and see what adventures lie ahead. More than once I have heard something like, "Being fired was the best thing that ever happened to me. It gave me the chance to do what I really wanted." For me the experience was just that, although it was a training exercise, and I hope it will be for you.

Turn being fired into your new chance even if you are faced with a "nicely done" moment.

If You Are Going to Get Fired, Get Fired Fast

The decision is made. If you really screwed up and did something that warrants being fired, then take your medicine and get out of there as fast as you can. Start wondering what the reference calls may reveal and hope that they stick to company policy: "Yes, he/she worked here and that is all I can tell you."

Most of us get fired for other reasons or no reason. Some phrase like "business downturn" will be invoked. Another handy one is "restructuring and your job is being eliminated." Sometimes it is for bad performance, but no matter. You don't need to commiserate with the boss; take the severance check, clean out your cubicle, turn in your badge, and get out of there. Nothing will be gained by sticking around or trashing the boss's car—you won't get the job back. Start thinking and planning for the next job; it's an opportunity.

If you are one of the many who are now fired via e-mail, all of the above applies, only faster.

When Resigning, Do It Fast

The other day someone asked me if he could see me on Friday afternoon, and it would only take a minute. I didn't need any more hints; I knew this person was going to resign. And, sure enough, he did.

Over the course of a career I have accepted bunches of resignations and I have resigned myself. Now I know there is a right way and a wrong way to do it.

The right way to do it is—quickly. Resignations shouldn't take long. Be appreciative and never, ever burn any bridges. You will be surprised where your boss and coworkers show up later.

The temptation is to repair all the ills of the organization on your way out. You have a list of things you would fix if you were in charge. Plus, there is the dreaded exit interview, the perfect opportunity to recommend all the fixes and, hey, while we're at it, let's throw the boss under the bus. Don't do it. You are on your way out, you are looking forward to your next gig.

The right way to do it is—as fast as possible. Both getting canned and quitting shouldn't take long, five minutes at most. Get it over with and get over it. Once you are fired, the organization will probably treat you like you are dead. Once you quit, the organization treats you like a traitor at best and probably wonders why a traitor would want to hang around. So you become a dead traitor. May as well leave. Believe it or not, they will survive and maybe thrive, either way. Whether the company thrives or dies without you is no longer your concern. Never, never burn any bridges and move on after the five minutes are up.

I Don't Love You Anymore

No, it's not about love. I am talking about resigning from a job.

Happy is the case that you can resign with a new job in hand. Joy abounds. You went through a very difficult decision-making process and it is now time for a change. You made the decision and there must be lots of reasons, so stick with it. The bloom is off the rose, you've lost that loving feeling and it won't come back. But then, cognitive dissonance kicks in when the "old" employer tries to talk you out of it.

I was once talked out of quitting and regretted it immediately. Sure, there was a little more money but it was still the same job and still the same boss. Nothing else had changed so I ended up quitting again and felt worse the second time. It was like the time my high school girlfriend talked me out of breaking up with her. The next day I regretted it and it was even worse a week later when I broke up with her again. The second time she was prepared to deal with me with a vengeance.

If you are accepting the resignation, make it quick from your end too. Don't try to talk anyone out of it. It will only be a matter of time before the person quits again.

Never get talked out of quitting by your boss, even if there is more money.

How to Fire a CEO

CEOs are fired all the time. Most don't like it but generous severance packages make it easier. So most don't say anything and go off to be CEO somewhere else, or they "retire," or they leave because they want to spend more time with the family. CEOs don't appreciate being fired, although they rarely hesitate when it comes time to fire others. The fired CEO is embarrassed, humiliated, and now might have to be reconsidered for the country club membership. And, even though no CEO should be surprised when the ax comes down (there are always plenty of clues, like stock performance), the fired CEO has a variety of communications styles and reactions.

Depending on the details of the separation agreement, some CEOs will talk to the press about how they were terminated unfairly and the process sucked, and they may even use the f-bomb. CEOs especially don't like to be fired via email, the telephone, or through the press and will note that indignity as necessary.

Others will send out a note to employees about the ouster, in which they describe accomplishments and bright futures.

We all work hard and we all believe that, in return, the least that our organizations owe us is respect and dignity. At the very least, a little courtesy is welcome, even when we are getting fired. Getting fired or resigning through Twitter is not okay.

Bridges can be burnt from both ends.

Lunch Is Neither a Good Time to Fire Someone nor to Get Fired

It was a nice restaurant that catered to the business lunch crowd. I was sitting there enjoying a nice lunch with one of my colleagues, celebrating some recent successes. All was good.

The tables were close and I wasn't listening closely, but I could overhear the guys at the table next to us discussing their families and plans for the business next year. I would glance over every once in a while as they were being served their salads and joking around. Just as coffee was served, there was a commotion at the table and a grown man started sobbing.

What an awkward situation. Whatever we call it, one poor guy had been fired by his lunch date. Terminated. Let go. Axed. After gaining his composure, the guy who lost his job shot off an expletive and bolted out of the restaurant.

I suspect neither will go back to that restaurant ever again. I am not sure I will ever return either. Too bad, I liked that restaurant.

Losing one's job is hard enough, don't spoil meals and give restaurants a bad name too. Some things are best done in the office.

What Kind of Gone Is Your Job?

Layoffs at one time meant you might be called back. Furloughed meant something temporary too. Both layoff and furlough now mean gone for good. Any recession could mean that once things get better, the job might come back. Maybe. Reduction in force means things are bad, set your expectations. Job eliminations mean robots are on the way. Fired always means fired.

We know some jobs are gone for good and for some, good riddance. For some that were moved to the nether regions offshore, we hear they may be coming back. That could be good if they are not really gone but I am not sure they are really coming back. Some were never gone in the first place because they are new, like all the green/sustainability-related jobs.

What is important to remember, no matter the job, is that it could be gone tomorrow and you need to be prepared for the next thing.

How you get "gone" is changing through technology. RadioShack sent an e-mail to a few thousand people telling them they were gone. So did Yahoo and a bunch of other big organizations. At least everyone hears at the same time and it is efficient. Just don't make the message pink. Pink slips don't convert to pink e-mails. The bad news about e-mail notifications is that not everyone is the same. The twenty-four-year-old who would like some time off probably welcomes one less trip to the office. The person who has been at the company for twenty-four years has a different perspective, like, "I gave them the best years of my life and this is the reward I get?"

It's a tricky situation at all levels. If you are worried about your job, you probably should be worried.

The Use of F-Bombs Won't Help You with Your Next Job

When you've been fired, the f-word often comes to mind. It may be okay for a minute. Go ahead, get it out of the way. In general, the f-word is not your friend at work. Even when others use it, you should reserve its use for outside the workplace, if at all. Sometimes it seems the only word that might suit the situation but find another one anyway.

Even when an interviewer uses the word, which should make you wonder about the organization he or she represents, stay away from it. Never let your guard down.

Think of how you would look in front of your mom or dad if you used the word.

When Terminated, Pay Less Attention to Delivery Mode Than to Content

We all know the story—it's only the characters that change. The story goes: "He (or she) worked here for twenty-five years, and they let him go through e-mail without any warning." Feelings are hurt. The prevailing thought is, if it happened to him, it could happen to me. Yes, harsh as it sounds, it could happen to you. Chances are, it *will* happen to you. When it does happen, you may be livid about the notification method, but the method is now the least of your worries. Once you soothe your crushed ego, your concerns should shift quickly to more important issues, like: What is the financial package? How long will my benefits be covered? Do I get to keep my computer? How long will my e-mail be operational? What about accrued sick leave and vacation time? Most organizations have lots of experience letting people go, so they should have the answers to all of these questions ready. This is the time to pay attention to the answers.

Our phones now tell us if the flight is late, if the table is ready, if the bank account is overdrawn, or if a tornado is coming. The phone will soon tell you, too, if your job has been eliminated. Ouch. The difference between inefficient and insensitive is razor thin. The message is less important than the details of severance benefits and benefits continuance.

Getting fired through Twitter may be inevitable. Just hope the tweet isn't for you anytime soon.

It Is Not Difficult to Get Fired—It Is Difficult to Get Hired Again

A friend of mine just got fired, and he was shocked. "I can't believe it!" he yelled. I know he worked for a thriving start-up company so when I asked him why, he just mumbled an answer. That mumble led me to believe that he was fired FOR CAUSE, aka, he did something stupid.

Contrary to the headlines on any given day, the rules for getting fired are pretty clear these days and they are ruthlessly enforced. Nonetheless, people are terminated every day for breaking the rules. I think some have a death wish when it comes to work.

Some seem to make a career out of getting fired. For those uninitiated who want to get fired, here are some surefire ways to get it done quickly:

Go AWOL. Just disappear with no excuse. You will be missed for about an hour before the pink slip hits your e-mail.

Or you could use your work computer to watch your favorite porn site.

There is always the time-tested technique of taking a weapon to work.

Maybe you could just tell a racist, sexist, homophobic, or crude joke that offends everyone.

Then there are the ambiguously worded rules about "inappropriate relations" or, more simply put, having sex with a subordinate.

If these tips are not helpful, just check out the daily news; it is full of good samples every day. It is not difficult to get fired if you just put your mind to it.

Never Resign Before Landing Another Job

You have had it. The boss is a jerk. The commute is giving you hemorrhoids. The chair in your work space is broken. The coffee that spews out in the office kitchen is toxic. It is time to quit. Wait a minute, don't do it. Get the next job first, no matter how long it takes.

Several reasons come immediately to mind. The paycheck looms large in this process. As in, if you quit without a new job there will be no paycheck for who knows how long. Another big reason is that it is easier to find a new job when you have a job. Without a current job, future employers want to know what happened and will almost always give the benefit of the doubt to the employer. Were you hard to work with? Were you really fired? What is your problem?

Even in a boom market, you cannot tell how long it will take to find that new job. Could be days, weeks, months, or worse. No matter how much workplace torture, keep the job and ramp up the new job hunt.

Besides, what could be a better feeling than telling the boss you have a great new job and he or she cannot talk you out of it.

My Career Clock Is Ticking

Career timelines are as critical as career choices.

First, there is the notion that "If I don't do it now, I will never be able to do it..." Think of the traditional entry-level jobs post-college or careers that require you to be a certain age. Big accounting firms mostly hire people right out of college. After a certain age you are no longer eligible to be a Navy Seal. You are only able to do those jobs at a young age. If you know what you want to do, don't let calendar avoidance eliminate your pursuit of a dream.

Other parts of the career timeline are important too. While I was chatting with a friend about her future, she said impatiently, "My career clock is ticking." She went on to explain, "I only have one or two jobs left in me, I better get out there if I am going to accomplish what I want." She was working backward from retirement, not looking forward from college.

Most of us are somewhere between right out of college and working backward from retirement but the career timeline principle still applies. Who does a career timeline apply to and when? Answer is, everyone and all the time. Here's why:

- Entry-level jobs can stay entry level for a long, long time if you are not careful. Sometimes a move is necessary to get past the new kid on the block. Break out of those "entry-level" jobs as soon as you can and accelerate your timeline.

- Mid-level career jobs can be a waste of talent if you are not careful. It's easy to get stuck. And, when you are "stuck," it is easy to be eliminated when there is a downsizing. If you have ever uttered the phrase, "By this point in my career I thought I would be further along," you need to ask yourself very tough questions. Are you doing what you want to do? Are you making a difference? Most importantly, how long have you been at this and how long do you want to do this? It may be time to see if your career timeline will allow you to do other things.

■ Everyone reaches a point where he or she is no longer preparing for the next thing. At some point, you are not preparing for graduate school. You are not preparing for a "real" job. You are not preparing for what you really want to do. As one friend put it, "I am no longer rehearsing for the next thing." If that's the case and the preparation is over, is this where you want to be?

■ Self-assessment is always useful. Gauge where you are relative to where you want to be for your age. If you are on target or way ahead, no changes may be needed. If you are way behind it might be time to plot out the career timeline and make changes.

When it comes to your career, are you working from a timeline? If not, put a little thought into where you are, where you want to be, and what is left. The timeline can guide you more than you think.

Moving from Boy Wonder to the Gray Hair in the Room

Age plays a big part in the workplace. Once I was the boy wonder; now I am called on when we need some gray hair. It seemed there was very little in between.

Given all the emphasis in the workplace today on social media and technology, old age comes faster than it used to and is more limiting. Experience may not be your friend because it means you are old. Discrimination based on age, however discreet, is the big elephant in the room in most organizations. We don't talk about it but it lurks around every cubicle corner. It is illegal and it is only behind closed doors that the topic is even mentioned.

You can be angry about it. You can dye your hair. You can carry a backpack and wear hoodies. You can eliminate all dates on your resume. People can still approximate your age. Eliminate as many clues as you can but recognize that age is a part of the decision-making process at work. The only advantage to getting older regarding work is that you know more people and you have more relationships, and that might be the most important asset of all.

Is It Too Late?

So much attention is showered on billionaires who are barely out of college that it would be easy to resign yourself to a mediocre career or settle for something for which you have no passion. Even though riches and accolades are heaped on the twenty-three-year-old, it is never too late. A forty-year-old is not an old geezer. Ideas and passion do not have expiration dates.

Bob Noyce founded Intel when he was forty-one. John Pemberton invented Coca-Cola when he was fifty-five. Colonel Sanders was sixty-five when he started KFC. So for all of you who are thinking of something big, of making a change, of starting something, the world has not passed you by. Your ideas are still worthy. It is never too late.

As the Chinese proverb proclaims, "The best time to plant a tree was twenty years ago. The second best time is today."

The Make More Money Thing

Want to make more money? Do a great job and ask for a raise. If you lack the gumption to do that, here are some creative ideas.

1. **Read *People* magazine for inspiration.** You will see that those with no talent, no skills, and no job can grow rich and famous. There is hope for all of us.

2. **Create a personal and imaginary board of directors.** Remember those imaginary friends you had when you were little? Bring them back, except this time make them the people you would LIKE to turn to for advice. When faced with an issue, ask, "What would Paul Newman do? Or Oprah Winfrey? Or my first mentor?" Their advice is always very helpful.

3. **Borrow a puppy and walk around the places where business-people congregate.** The number of connections you have will grow exponentially. The connections may lead to a better-paying job. Be sure to give the puppy back.

4. **Never roll your eyes over an idea.** That response, even once, will stop people from sharing ideas with you. With no ideas to borrow or share, you might be stuck with only your own ideas and not move ahead in the organization.

5. **Be the person your dog thinks you are.** You will succeed beyond your own expectations and make bundles of money.

6. **Get off Facebook.** Unless you work at FB, chances are you are wasting time looking at quotes from the Dalai Lama or photos of happy people. If you used that time for doing your job, you might get a raise.

7. **Collect people every day.** Business is all about developing relationships. Relationships don't flourish if you never leave your cube or never look up from your phone. Get out, do something, meet people; the relationships you form are your currency.

8. **Do not travel.** When you travel you never capture all of your expenses, plus you waste money. And by God, since you are traveling, you deserve that drink or that large bag of gummy bears.

Given the economic realities, we all may have to be pretty creative to make more money. It's not just about salary.

That Personal Brand Thing

No one should be without a personal brand. Or at least that is what everyone is telling us. The guy in the cubicle down the hall told me he spent all weekend working on his personal brand, and I wonder what he did. When I hear about branding my mind heads toward Super Bowl commercials and Bud Light and Pringles and trying to sell more all the time. If we have a personal brand, what are we selling? What does it mean? If we don't have one, should we feel guilty? Are we failures?

Stars like Homer Simpson and Elvis Presley have personal brands. I get that, and those brands are well deserved. But why does the guy down the hall who talks to his girlfriend all day need a personal brand? He says his brand will navigate him into future success. Good look on him.

There are books, blogs, newsletters, seminars, and coaches all about personal branding. There is an entire branding industry. But, like potato chips or diet soda, where it's hard to tell one from another, if everyone has a personal brand how will anyone know who is special and who is not?

Maybe it will be about who makes the most noise. Better start working on that brand.

What Do You Do?

It shouldn't be a difficult question. But for a lot of us, the question "What do you do?" is more complicated than it should be. Unless you are a doctor, lawyer, or rock star, the answer to the question might be more than people want to know.

How do you answer the question easily if you are a bunker fuel purchase coordinator or a flux capacitor designer?

The question is posed at schools, on airplanes, at cocktail parties—everywhere! My mother even asks me.

The best interchange I've had on the question just happened. In a hotel lobby a young concierge asked me, "What do you do?" Rather than go into any details, I replied, "Oh, a little of this and a little of that."

He said, "I used to do that, but now I am doing this. I plan to do this until the next that comes up. This is good for now but I wish I had a better handle on what that will be."

What a great way to say, "I don't know, but this is good for now."

Start All Over!

Lots of habits are formed in college. Other habits at work just develop through routine and by acting like trained killer whales. Dare I say it? Some of those habits are not good ones. So my advice is to start all over. Dump those habits with resolve, and look at life with the attitude, "It's a brand new day!"

You may be asking, what habits did I develop and how do I repent? Rather than focus on the bad habits, let me focus on the cure that will ensure career success and happiness. Here is the very short list:

First, get up early. For the college graduate, the habit you need to break is sleeping until the lunch bell rings. The day in the "real world" does not begin at 12:30 p.m. The successful people I have been around are ready to go when the rooster is crowing.

Second, read! For many of you, reading is a chore, something that needs to be done only to meet a requirement and be compliant. Habits of dreading time spent reading or only doing the minimum might have been formed at an early age. Abandon that thought and start over with a renewed sense of the wonders of reading a good book. Interesting people are successful and interesting people read.

Dump the nickname. Nicknames are common in any group, including your family, and nicknames tend to stick. Fifty years from now, classmates or family members will greet you by your long-lost nickname whether you want them to or not. And the range of nicknames can run from the forgettable to the unfortunate to the "wish I could get rid of this nickname."

So for those of you graduating with the nickname Jimbo or Scooter, you have nothing to worry about with a sticky nickname. For those of you with names like Big Lebowski, Party Girl, Dancing Fool, or any other name that is the result of what might be one wayward night of ill-conceived activities, rejoice. Until the next reunion, you have an opportunity to kick that ill-gained and less-wanted moniker.

But don't blow the opportunity, because the workplace is full of nicknames too. Before you get trapped in one for your career, here is a list of the ten work nicknames to avoid:

1. **Homer.** Yes, that Homer. Homer Simpson may be lovable and he may be the character from which people in faraway lands form their opinions of American men, but he is not your model for work performance. Picture him at the nuclear plant. You don't want your coworkers concerned about the equivalent of nuclear meltdown at your new gig.

2. **Zoom Zoom.** Pace and rhythm are very important at work. Going too fast can be just as bad as going too slow. If you are out of step with the rest of the team, they will go after you.

3. **Attila.** The list of names that describes Attila the Hun–type behavior is long. None of them is good. It means that the work gets done but there could be dead bodies along the way. Not good.

4. **Grumpy.** One of the Seven Dwarfs who is not fun to be around. On second thought, none of the names of the dwarfs is good. Happy might be the exception.

5. **Bozo, Crusty, or any clown name.** This one is self-explanatory.

6. **Meeting King or Queen.** No one likes meetings. Don't be the one who is always calling for them.

7. **Phantom.** If this is your nickname, you might not ever know it because you are not around to hear anyone call you by it. Working from home has created more than a few "Phantoms."

8. **Diva.** Man or woman, you know who you are and what that means.

9. **Ken or Barbie.** It's good to always look good at work, but not that good. Don't be perfect. If all your coworkers look forward to mussing up your hair, you are not quite fitting in.

10. **Pigpen.** Picture your room in college. Now resolve you will never operate out of a space that looks like that again.

There you have it, the list of work nicknames to avoid. The same list would apply to Twitter handles. It might be best to have no nicknames. Boy or Girl Wonder might be the exception.

So start all over. There are very few times where that option is a possibility, and starting a new job is one of those times.

That Ten Thousand–Hour Rule

Malcolm Gladwell is a business book hero, and he brought a new rule to the world that continues to spread.

It is the ten thousand–hour rule. It claims that if one does something for ten thousand hours, one should be really good at it. Examples are the Beatles and Bill Gates, to name a few. And who doesn't want to be the Beatles or Bill Gates?

Ten thousand hours is a long time. At work, it's at least five years. So if you have held your job for more than five years you should be pretty good at it.

If you are not good at it by ten thousand hours, you probably have a job you don't like and it might be time to change. Or, find a new career you love and start counting to ten thousand.

You could be the next Paul McCartney or Bill Gates.

The Work–Life Balance Thing

Work–life balance is long gone. The contest between work and life is over—work won. Work didn't win because people are necessarily spending more time in the office or because we are more committed to the missions and visions hanging on the walls. Work is the champion because we are always "on" and proud of it. We are addicted to devices, and what's at the top of the screen? Work. Are we working when we check e-mail at 9:00 p.m.? Are we working when we are at the youth soccer game and listening to a conference call (while on mute) at the same time? The answer is, sort of.

In distinguishing between work and life, we tend to think of work as grinding it out on spreadsheets at the desk. Life, as defined in the equation, is sitting around the pool or picnicking with the family in wine country without a care in the world. Both work and life are probably in between those images. To many, the concept of balance is more about the outlets we create to escape from work, even for just a short while.

Outlets will range from mountain climbing to quiet time with a spouse or from reading to restoring that old Mustang convertible. All are appropriate and create that "life" part of the equation. But most outlets we create, like the ones I've mentioned, require planning, concentration, and communication. Those requirements sound like work. One outlet exists that is truly an activity that lets the mind relax and escape from work—trash TV.

No need to feel guilty about trash TV habits. I learned about its powers of rejuvenation from no less than the president of a distinguished Ivy League institution. The president was asked how to create a work–life balance in an environment that is always "on." Is it possible to find a life and retreat for even a short while? The answer the president gave was, "The secret to work–life balance is trash TV."

The message is that the secret to balance could be shutting down, even for a little while. And what more convenient vehicle to shutting down is there than trash TV? It's free and in your house right now. You don't have to do anything other than click the remote control. The definition of trash TV is very individual and no judgment need be a part of your choice. The choices are infinite and could include *American Idol, The Real Housewives of New Jersey,* or *Seinfeld* reruns. Sometimes your brain just needs to shut down and let someone else do the work.

Your own version of trash TV does not even need to include a television. Trash TV is a metaphor for downtime. True downtime might include spending time with the kids with no plan and no device to check. Or a long walk without talking about or thinking about work. Or looking out the window at the birds. You can choose, but for most of us, that downtime without any work is a key part of the "life" part of work–life balance.

When the brain is rejuvenated through activities like trash TV, you are more likely to be ready to go back to work and fight the good fight. You are more likely to perform better.

Outlets are an important part of the work world. The outlets are not always the kind you plug your many devices into, so you don't have to worry about power. Maybe we should embrace the imbalance.

Homer Simpson would agree: trash TV is the way to save a career.

Not My Job

A relic that continues to persist in the office is the job description. Sure, employees need to know what they are supposed to do when they show up, but the phrase "That's not my job" disappeared a while ago.

Anyone who wanted to *keep* his job learned that. The job description that limits you may be gone, but a few definitions at work shouldn't be hard.

The three questions we all want to know at work are simple, whether you are a CEO or on the lower end of the spectrum. They are:

- What's my job?
- How am I doing?
- How does my effort make a difference around here?

If you can answer these three questions you are pretty lucky. If you can't answer today, work on it and tell your boss. He or she probably has the same questions.

Sounds pretty simple, but most organizations have a hard time answering them. No job descriptions required, just answers to three simple questions.

The Job Title Thing

Job titles are like political speeches—some of them sound good but you don't know the meaning. Job titles are a big deal and the cause of angst and glory, even though a title may not change a life very much.

Some organizations that are woefully lacking in the innovation department are very creative when it comes to job titles. The really confusing job titles seem to be an attempt to placate an unhappy person by creating a title that no one understands. A new title is a lot cheaper than a raise.

A favorite title I spotted is Senior Chief Principal for Strategy Organization Transformation Management. Then there is Mall Santa and Rasputin Impersonator. At least I know what Mall Santa and Rasputin Impersonator are supposed to do. Bunker Fuel Purchase Coordinator has a nice ring to it, as does Pile Butt. I really like Chief Garbologist, which has both an air of importance and trash at the same time.

A job title should be nothing more than a description of rank with a clue about what is entailed in the job, like Vice President of Manufacturing or Master Electrician. Getting worked up about a title is often a waste of emotional currency.

Projects, Projects, Projects

The skills required today to be successful are legion. Whenever I take a gander at the requirements to fill any job, I am on the verge of a panic attack.

No matter the job, there are technical skills, communication skills, people skills, storytelling skills, relationship skills. I saw one spec that required the ability to differentiate quadratic equations in your head. WHOA. It is a very long list that can intimidate any job seeker.

The lists are so long it is hard to discern the most important skill one needs in today's workplace. So I will let you in on the secret.

The most important skill you need today is project management. The person who can demonstrate that she can effectively manage a project will get a job and get ahead. That is, the person who can start the project, keep people engaged during the tough times, and then bring it to a positive closure will be a hero to the boss and colleagues.

Be a hero, manage a project.

The Networking Thing

Networking is the name of the game. All roads, websites, blogs, and parental advice lead to the importance of networking. Networking is the secret sauce that can allow you to swap out that terrible job with an asshole boss for one that is unbelievably exciting and rewarding with headquarters near the beach.

Need a few million dollars for that start-up idea? Network!

All the social sites, such as LinkedIn and Facebook, are efficient ways to network. The trick is to know how to use them for networking.

Someone sent me an e-mail the other day with a request to touch base to pick my brain. Maybe we could even break a bagel, he said.

I don't need another bagel and my brain was picked long ago. But—and it's a big but—I might be willing to help him if he would tell me how I might help. The "how" is the key.

And that is the secret to networking. The networkee needs to understand what the networker wants. The request could be for an introduction, or it could be for advice, or it could be for a clandestine interview—just be clear what you want. (Regarding the clandestine interview, you can be coy about that one.)

People are almost always willing to help, it's just that no one wants their brain picked.

Talking About Pay!

What do we say about our own compensation? We are dying to know what everyone makes, but should we talk about it? It is an ultrasensitive topic. If we don't bring the topic up and ask questions, how will we know if we make more than the guy down the hall who is a real slacker?

Talk about a slippery slope, especially when women are usually on the short end of the pay stick. Lots of companies frown on any kind of sharing. And many people think it is just bad form to talk about money at all. One can be seen as either bragging or whining, and there is not much in between. It gets complicated, considering that there are lots of reasons that people don't necessarily make the same money. Experience, skill level, and being related to the boss all come into play.

The best ploy to find out about pay without blabbing is market research. Lots of compensation surveys are out there that can give you an idea if your pay is fair or not. If it's not fair, that's the time to raise money concerns. You have to ask and be ready for a no.

Real information about pay, not gossip, is a good thing.

Working in the Polar Vortex

Even in the dead of winter we have to show up for work. Snow days are long gone, since we can work remotely. Winter excuses are few. Even cars start when the temperature is way below zero. Showing up for work is one thing, but what happens when you are frozen out *at* work? The symptoms of being frozen out are obvious and include:

- No longer being included on e-mail distribution lists.
- Not being invited to meetings.
- Colleagues stop chatting with you in the coffee room.

Now what? Is there a hygiene problem? Do people think you are a jerk? Are you about to get fired and everyone knows it except you? If the answer is yes, you are a part of the corporate polar vortex and it is time to make changes.

The change involves whatever behavior, smell, or circumstance pushed you out into the cold in the first place. Change is always a difficult proposition but it could save you from a worse circumstance when you are thrown OUT into the cold.

Maybe by the time spring arrives you will have warmed up.

Is Work Killing Us?

Commitment and passion for your work is one thing. It can be rewarding and provide a sense of worth that we all crave. Work may also kill you. At least that is what some of the research is pointing out. Since we spend so much time at work, what happens there has an impact on mental and physical health.

What happens at work affects stress, and stress is the variable that impacts health. Harmful work circumstances can be a killer. Researchers are finding that toxic workplaces are as bad as smoking and obesity.

Work requires some soul-searching every Monday. Is it worth it?

What Happens on the Road Does Not Stay on the Road

The headline says it all. Being away from home or the office does not grant any special license for you to do anything you would not ordinarily do.

Availability Is Not a Skill

"We are desperate for someone to lead this group." So said the big-time executive. The company is in deep trouble and needs a person to lead the way out of the woods through a new initiative. There are thousands of worried people inside the company ready to do anything to save it. There are millions of people looking for a job, ready to join the company even if it is a sinking ship. *How hard can this be?* I thought. It was hard.

The process of finding someone for any role is pretty tried and true: write a job description, hire a search firm or give it to internal recruiting, and wait while they troll through the universe of likely candidates. Then we hope that someone guessed right on what is really needed in the job and hope that someone happened to be looking for a job at the same time. Assuming the lucky coincidence occurs, there are now candidates, and the interviews begin.

The process and the regular protocols for finding the right candidates do not necessarily work. Usually there is waiting. And waiting. And waiting. Meanwhile, nothing gets done. How can this be so hard?

So someone may finally emerge who everyone thinks can do the job. "Thinks" is the key word. In a perfect world, the person picked would be perfect. It is not a perfect world. "Good enough" is the phrase that often pops up. "Available" is the word that goes with "good enough." When combined, the two words create a witches' brew of talent.

Just because someone is available does not mean he or she is qualified. Frustrating as it might be, get the right person for the job. Conversely, just because you are available doesn't mean you should accept the job that is offered. Availability is not a skill.

Career Paths Are Accidents

Careers are defined by experience, preparation, schooling, and lots of luck and serendipity. There is rarely a clear path. It's more like running around through the bushes and the brambles than being on a path. To imply there are paths hurts the adventure.

Whoever put the two words "career" and "path" together should be whipped with wet noodles. The two words just do not go together. A career is a joyful journey filled with getting hired, getting fired, and other stops along the way. We pivot, we change, we repot the plant, we change our minds, we follow a passion, we need the money, we go after stock options, we change cities, we get promoted, we get disappointed, we get in trouble, we make lifelong friends, we worry if we are living up to our own expectations, and we wonder why we worry.

My own career is like most. It has been full of challenges and almost always full of excitement. The research points to the fact that we all want to derive a sense of meaning and purpose from our work. It is not easily done but it is something we should strive for. We should continue on the career journey until we feel like there is a sense of worth in what we do.

When I accepted my last job, I was told that I just rewrote the first sentence of my obituary. From a career perspective, there is no higher praise.

When Playing Hooky Is Okay

Playing hooky. In any language those are two words that conjure the notion of ditching high school and going to the beach or sneaking away with friends for other adventures. Playing hooky also means getting caught and paying the consequences. No one ever plays high school hooky without getting caught.

But what about work? Is it ever okay to play hooky from work? The stakes are a little higher than they were in high school and the consequences could be more severe. Just like in high school, chances are you will get caught playing work hooky too. Posting on Facebook or Instagram from the beach on a Tuesday is always a clue. Participating in a conference call with Jimmy Buffet music playing in the background is another big clue. Opinions vary greatly on this hooky workplace dilemma.

Is it ever okay to play hooky from work? Here are just a few questions that may arise: Is it okay to play hooky when your long-lost college friend is in town? Is it okay to play hooky when it's your birthday? Is it okay to play hooky to go shopping after you finish that big project? What about when the new Star Trek movie opens? Is it *ever* okay?

These are all judgment calls. Maybe yes, maybe no, depending on where you work, the nature of your job, and the tolerance level of your boss.

In some places, attendance is not as important as results. Too bad it's not that way in all places. These are the places that may not know what hooky is because people come and go and are trusted to do the right thing and get the job done. These are the places where people couldn't define hooky. In other places, showing up is about all that counts, and that means hooky can creep into the culture.

The next time you get the urge to play hooky, include these thoughts in your decision:

- Working from home is not playing hooky. Of course, that assumes you are working.
- When out of the office, keeping in touch is not the same as keeping tabs. Returning e-mails and voice mails all day is more like work than hooky.

- Letting your team down by not showing up when they need you is not hooky—it is desertion. Don't do it.
- Sometimes a workday is required to go to the dentist or the DMV, get the dog spayed, or do other chores that cannot be done over the weekend. None of this is fun so it's probably not hooky. It's life.
- If you are struggling to create a good excuse for the absence, it's probably hooky, and the excuse better be credible. My favorite is, "My father died and I had to paint the kitchen."

Sometimes hooky is just plain worth it. Or at least forty thousand people at a time may think so when your beloved baseball team is playing at home in the World Series. Occasionally, an event presents itself that makes normal people throw caution to the wind. Doing something that you will always remember might be worth the risk of a little hooky. Just don't get caught on the Jumbotron.

The bottom line is: if you know your worth to the organization is key and an occasional day off can boost your productivity over the long term, it is not hooky—it is clearing the mind for the next surge.

They Will Never Survive Without Me

How many times have we heard that sentiment? Everyone from CEOs down to those on the lowest rung of the organization chart at one time or another entertained that dangerous thought. The thought usually occurs when we are feeling put upon and we want to get even, with spite oozing out of every pore.

We work hard, we know how to get things done, we know where the skeletons are hidden and, GOSHDARNIT, they really need me!

Truth is, organizations are incredibly resilient and, yes, will survive without you just fine, no matter who you are. So the next time you are thinking smug thoughts and want to get even with "them," remember that no one is irreplaceable.

Do your best, enjoy your work, and don't be smug.

Are You Remarkable?

Studies are done every week about what makes someone special at work. Even more than special, we are talking about remarkable! To paraphrase thousands of studies, here is what remarkable people do:

Remarkable people ignore job descriptions. They do whatever it takes, regardless of role or position, to get things done.

Remarkable people are eccentric. People who aren't afraid to be different naturally stretch boundaries and challenge the status quo, and they often come up with the best ideas.

Remarkable people are generous. They recognize the contributions of others, especially in group settings where the impact of their words is even greater. They give help and advice. They are mentors and teachers.

So if you ignore things, and are eccentric and generous, congratulations, you are probably making a big impact. Keep pushing.

Whether or not your boss likes you is another question.

How to Get a Raise

I want a raise, you want a raise, we all want a raise, but no one wants to ask for one, including me. So how does one go about getting an increase in compensation?

A wise person once told me that the easiest way to get a raise is to work fewer hours. The logic implies that your personal hourly rate goes up. Working fewer hours is not often an option for those trying to get ahead and pump up that performance review. The solution may be as simple as listening to your mom, who probably still says, "If you don't ask, you don't get."

Experts say you should do two things: one is to "find the money-making tasks and do those." These are usually the most challenging or onerous tasks in the organization. Or, these are the roles that will generate revenue, like sales or product development.

The other way to get a raise is to meet with the boss and find out what it will take to get that raise. In so doing, you can develop a trusted relationship that could mean more money down the road.

And there is always that option of changing jobs to get that raise.

Sell, Baby, Sell

Career-planning classes are a staple in college and a lot of high schools these days. After identifying skills, interests, and aptitudes, one can make decisions about a bright future and live happily ever after. Except it doesn't quite work like that.

I am asked sometimes to speak to career-planning classes and I always ask the same question to kick off the session. The question is, "How many of you want to go into sales?" and I ask for a show of hands. The response is always the same—no one raises a hand.

I spend the remainder of the session telling the audience to Get Over It because we are *all* in sales. No one believes me so we then play a game— they name a profession and I explain how sales is a part of that career.

Doctor? Lawyer? Teacher? Marine biologist? Astronaut? Success in every career is rooted in some element of sales.

How Busy Are You?

What an impossible question. It's like the question, "When did you stop beating your spouse?" There is no good answer. When the boss asks the question, several thoughts spring to mind.

"Not very busy" is not a good response. That answer could lead to the boss wondering why you are around at all if there is not enough work for you to do. Alternatively, more work may be heaped on you if the belief is that you have excess capacity.

"Pretty busy" is an okay answer but sounds halfhearted and like you really don't want to do any more. It could lead to a belief that you don't care and that you are bringing morale down and having a negative impact on the culture.

A better answer might be, "I am crazy busy." But if you sound too busy you might miss out on working on that wildly interesting project that needs a sponsor.

The best answer is, "I am really busy but I always have room to do more to make us even more successful." Or something like that...

When you hear the question, alarms and fireworks should go off at the same time. Something good or bad is about to happen to you. No matter how you answer it, chances are good that more work is on the way. So get ready.

One Size Fits All?

My hat collection is growing. Everyone who works has a hat collection. Most are cheap "gimme" hats with Velcro snaps on the back that are given out at events like picnics and the day at the ballpark. Some hats are real ones with sizes on the back. It is not unusual to see baseball caps stacked on top of each other somewhere in a cubicle. Most hats feature corporate logos above the brim and some have more to say, like "SALES KICKOFF 2020" or "People Are Our Business."

My own collection of corporate hats is in perfect condition because none of them fits. I have a big head. My mother always said it means I am really smart and my head is big to hold all those brains. What it really means is that the promise that "One Size Fits All" is a big fat lie. The hats are all too small for me to wear but I keep collecting them.

Why can't organizations learn from hats? When it comes to almost every decision that involves the lives and well-being of people, one size does not fit all. Instead, we all try to squeeze into a hat that is too small or we flop around in one that is too big.

While I wait for organizations to be more flexible, I would like to have a hat that fits.

Wait Until Your Father Gets Home

The thing is, he is home. There are more stay-at-home dads than ever in the history of the world. The reasons that dads are staying home are as varied as the types of dads. It could be that dad can't find a job or cannot work. Or, maybe there are special-needs children who require dad to be home. Or, maybe mom has a much better job than dad and she is the breadwinner.

It is easier to work than it is to be home with the kids.

Regardless of the reasons, the fact that dads are home with kids is changing the workplace and the kids. The perception of dads at home is changing too. No longer shy and a little weird, the guys are right in there at the schools and parks.

There could be another big reason that dad is home with the kids. He might like them.

Saying Versus Hearing

What is said and what is heard at work are rarely the same thing. If we had a split screen of a conversation between two people, the difference between said and heard would be startling. I just heard the difference in action at an airport while eavesdropping.

Guy #1 (the one I can hear) opened the call happily with, "Happy Thursday, partner!" Who says "partner"?

Guy #2, on the other end, is already on red alert. What he heard was, "Something is about to happen to me."

Guy #1 continues, "Say, I wanted to give you a heads up. You interviewed for that big job really well but we are giving the job to someone else."

What Guy #2 heard is, "You are a loser."

The chat went on with buzzwords like "sell through" and "market penetration" sprinkled in. But make no mistake, it was a coldhearted rejection delivered from a cell phone at an airport with lots of background noise. The interaction was a good reminder for me of how sensitive we all need to be in understanding the difference between what we say and what is heard.

The call wrapped up when Guy #1 said, "I'll be coming out to work with you soon and we can go out to get a beer."

What Guy #2 thought was, "Fat chance. If I see you in the parking lot I may speed up to hit you." Listen carefully.

Feedback Follies

When it comes to feedback at work, most people say they crave it. They all lie.

As one manager told me recently, "Everyone says they want feedback, but the part they leave off is that they only want feedback if it is positive."

Feedback might be the most important element of improving performance at work. But the best feedback is rarely given because no one wants to hurt feelings or be known as the jerk boss. It's a problem in the workplace today. We all walk on eggs when it comes to the area of "needs improvement."

Remember those tough teachers you had in high school. You may not have liked them but they made you better. Remember that coach who said, "Not good enough." And you improved.

Yes, get all the feedback you can, but get the bad with the good. It's the shortest way to get a raise and promotion.

Sex, Listening, and Other Considerations

"We had sex on my desk over the weekend." So said the new vice president to all of us who reported to him. We were working at a video game maker and we were seated around said desk. It was a Monday morning and we had been anxious while we were waiting for him to appear. He was new and we were told he would shake things up, that he was creative, and that he thinks outside the box. Apparently, he thinks on top of the desk, and thanks for sharing.

The guy seemed pretty normal as he described his "results-oriented" style and the importance of open communications. Blah, blah, blah. Nothing new there. But the meeting quickly plummeted into unknown territory.

There were no telltale signs of fun and games. There were no half-empty champagne glasses or Barry White CDs tossed around. In fact, the desk was full of stuff—the guy's desktop computer and books and photos of his children were all about. We silently wondered how they managed around all the regular desk stuff. We also wondered if there must be some sort of company policy that prohibits sex on desks on weekends.

The new vice president read our minds. "Don't worry," he said, "the company believes what you do on your own time is not regulated." I wondered if anyone else in the company would ever use that desk again. And if so, will they know what happened on it? "And I believe in that philosophy too," he said. "What you do on your own time is none of my business and you can be whoever you want to be outside of the office." We looked around at one another in a new light, expecting to see pimps and ax murderers.

He went on, "There is a reason why I had sex on my desk with my wife yesterday. You see, I believe I will spend so much time in the office away from her, I want to have her essence and spirit with me while I am working. We christen every office I will work in." Well, that explains it and it makes perfect sense. He was unabashed and unapologetic in his belief that coitus near the cubicles was a good thing. While we were all trying to absorb what he had just announced, he shifted the topic and wanted each of us to declare what our individual goals were for the next quarter. Although not declared, one goal each of us resolved was to never go near his desk again.

After the disclosures by the new vice president, no one ever looked at him as a leader. He was viewed more as a slimy guy no one wanted to be near, let alone have lunch with. He never gained any respect and within six months he was gone. Maybe he just quit all of his jobs so he could "christen" a new desk.

In today's organization, being describes as "creative" can run the gamut from "interested in design" to just plain "crazy." In earlier days the range was only from very corporate to very casual. Leadership gurus all recommend being genuine and letting those around you know who you are— share your true self. But it can go too far. Being genuine can turn into wimpy if you are not careful about the "genuine" parts you are sharing. And letting colleagues know much about the intimacies of your private life is downright weird. Sharing anything intimate is sharing too much.

I would recommend not having sex on your desk, but if you do, I would not share it. There is that whole video thing...

Sharing Too Much Can Become a Habit

Two kinds of people show up on your social media feed: those who lead perfect lives and want everyone to know about it and those who post videos of kittens and inspirational messages and want you to know that they don't have a job.

Sharing can morph from a vice to a habit. And, what you do on social media can define you but maybe not in the way you want.

Not everything needs to be shared.

Pornography Is Not Your Friend

Study after study finds that a large percentage of Internet use involves pornography. Shocking. I suspect that more than one of those users is sitting in a workplace and being paid. I would guess, too, that any research study's demographics would show that men are more likely than women to be peeking at the nasty sites. Guys can only play video games for so long, and then what? The answer is, not learning a new language.

When I received a call from a client at 8:05 a.m. one day, I knew it would not be good news. To meet deadlines, the junior consultants are often the ones who bear the brunt of burning the midnight oil. And the night before the call from the client we had an entire team of twenty-four-year olds sitting in cubes under fluorescent lights doing spreadsheets or something like that. One of the young guys was more bored than the others. He took it upon himself to download some raunchy pornography. The first problem was that he was using the client's computer. The second problem was that he sent the porn that he had downloaded to a few hundred of his friends with his own commentary attached. The third problem was that the company where he was sitting monitors all computer activity with a special eye on anything with the words "blonde," "young," or "MILF" in the title.

When I called said porn distribution captain into my office, he readily admitted that he needed a mental break from the tedium of looking at numbers so he went the way of porn. Couldn't he have played *Pac-Man* for a minute? I gave him credit for being so honest but then told him to pack his bags, that he was being terminated, and that he was, as of that moment, a free agent. He was shocked. He wanted a second chance.

Some rules that are broken are so egregious that there are no second chances. Most rules related to pornography are in that category.

Love in the Elevator

Aerosmith may have had success with the song "Love in an Elevator," and the band may in fact have had love in the elevator, but that was before video cameras were everywhere. Or maybe rock stars seek out videos in elevators. For anyone at work, love in the elevator would result in being met by security when the elevator doors finally open. Then, probably termination.

Video cameras are everywhere now and are not necessarily easy to spot. Need an example of an act caught on video? An executive was agitated that someone had parked in his reserved parking place in the company parking lot. So agitated that he "keyed" the car that was parked there. When confronted by security he denied it, but the event was caught on tape. The executive was terminated for lying.

Another executive who was about to resign wanted to secretly move out of her office over a weekend in order to avoid confrontation. Once again, smile, you're on camera.

Thinking about stealing office supplies, trashing the boss's office, using the copier for the grammar school program, beating up your girlfriend, bringing cows up the stairs to surprise everyone on Monday morning? Think again, someone is watching.

No place is safe from video—parking lots, hallways, cafeterias, department stores, lobbies, sidewalks. Or, maybe every place is safer because of the videos. Videos just reinforce the adage that whatever you do, you will get caught, even if it takes time.

It's Best Not to Be Seen Naked by Colleagues

Sure, there's a world-class gym at the office and it's free. Do the workout—it will make you more productive and healthier. Just be alert about where and when you shower. You only want coworkers to know so much about you.

Naming Children Is Not a Spectator Sport

I love birth announcements. Each one is a billboard of happiness and hope and joy. One thing I've noticed on announcements in the Internet era is that, well, the names are a little weird. Gone are John and Susan. Traditional names are being replaced by names full of unusual combinations of letters adding up to names I've never heard before. The middle names can stretch to make another two or three unrecognizable words.

Don't assume unusual names are based on proud family heritage. One parent told me excitedly, "We named Zrxkin based on the URL availability. We made the name up and reserved the domain for the baby. It will help him later with his personal brand."

This makes total sense. Why not get the infant thinking about the future early? The Ivy League may be impressed.

So next time you hear that unusual newborn name, don't be too fast to judge, those parents may not be thinking about baby presents; they might be thinking about web presence.

Why Doesn't Anyone Listen to Me?

Walk into any cool, early-stage company in any city in the world and you won't see cubicles. You won't see offices. What you might see are dogs running around, bricks and old timbers, and hip young people in work spaces. But I doubt you are going to hear much chatter. Everyone is wearing headphones and listening to anything other than what is going on around them. Other than the faint sound of Pink Floyd, the scene is quiet and a little eerie.

What about team building and camaraderie? How do you make friends? How does communication happen? What about working together to better serve the organization? All of these things still matter at work. These are the things that make us like our job better and be more effective.

In any given all-employee survey the results will always highlight communication as the number-one issue in the organization. A large company I know once sent out daily communiqués to employees and everyone still screamed about the lack of communication. Managers have often wondered if they are heard by others, and with the universal spread of headphones, now they really wonder.

But maybe this is really not about communication at all. Even while wearing headphones people are communicating through texts and e-mail. As one tech exec put it, headphones are the new cubicles because they separate the work spaces.

Headphones are here to stay, so get a good pair and find the music genre that helps you be productive. Just don't forget to communicate.

Love and Hate Relationships

Love and hate relationships are not necessarily about your boss or that hottie on the fourth floor. We all have a love and hate relationship with our smartphone. We love that we can Skype with the kids while on a business trip but hate that we are constantly connected, even when on vacation. Is there hope for striking a balance in the love–hate balance? Maybe.

Treat mobility as a luxury that allows us to always be on but never be off. Therein lie the love and the hate. To be always on is to be responsive and always in touch. The hate part is the *same* side of the coin. We are obsessed about being out of touch, and organizations will let us be "on" as much as we choose to be.

Chances are better that the messages you are receiving skew toward the negative. The boss piles on some new work or you were outbid on eBay or the Nigerian prince who has billions needs your credit card number. A quick check of messages can ruin a nice evening. A message from a stranger can be a buzzkill, and the chances that you will receive a message that you won the lottery are slim.

One recent study found that, given the option, a large percentage of people would give up sex before they would give up their smartphone. Another report says that the average frequency with which people check their mobile device is every four minutes; that sounds like an addiction.

Addictions run the gamut from smoking to eating Big Macs to watching *Seinfeld* reruns. Now checking for messages on the phone is in that category and this addiction is here to stay. If you take even a small break from looking down at your phone, you might make a new friend, get promoted, or not get hit by a car.

Smartphones are a wonder of the universe. It's the device that lets us tap into the wisdom of the centuries, lets us find our way in the dark, gives us directions, answers questions, takes zillions of photos, and so much more. It's the invention that really has changed the world.

Let's love the good part of mobility and learn to deal with the hate part.

A View into Work

The world is full of only two types of people—those who are on LinkedIn and those who will be on LinkedIn. I like LinkedIn because we know that everyone on there is looking for a job or wants something. No apologies. The "wants something" crowd includes those who want an investment, a sale, an introduction, or a job, although few are willing to admit it. The real value in LinkedIn is that it provides a daily microscope of what is going on in the work world.

The rules about the workplace are changing so fast that everyone is looking for advice. Plus, Richard Branson tells us how to be successful and Arianna Huffington tells us how to be important. You don't have to take the advice but it sure is interesting.

Beware the Buttons

The workplace is governed by buttons. When you arrive at work the first button you might push is the close-the-elevator-doors button. (If you don't know by now, 85 percent of those buttons are not connected to anything.) Then there are all those buttons on your phone calling out to make you more productive or play a game. The coffee machine is full of so many buttons that make it look like a nuclear reactor. To actually get coffee produced is a small victory over technology.

But the computer on and off button is the one that signals the beginning and end to the day.

My favorite button of all is the DELETE button. Nothing says closure or "I am so focused I am not going to deal with this" more than that delete button. Hitting the delete key may be the most closure you get all day, so take a little joy each time you hit it.

What IS Business Casual?

An invite to a special event arrived in the mail and at the bottom in bold italics was the announcement, *Attire: Business Casual.*

Business casual used to be easy for me and other men. All it took was a blue blazer, khaki pants, and a blue shirt. It was an outfit that worked every time and one could wear it every day. Noooo problem. And women could wear the same thing, sort of.

Even though most events are business casual, my definition is not automatic anymore. I showed up at an event at a start-up company with my usual business casual on and everyone looked at me like I was the crazy college professor. Everyone else was wearing blue jeans and a black T-shirt. And there were dogs running around.

I think we need new categories that outline a little more than just plain business casual. More specific categories would take all the guessing out of what to wear. Here are a few suggestions that I would like to see at the bottom of an invitation:

- Dress like Steve Jobs did—blue jeans, mock black turtleneck, and hip eyeglasses. Works in most places.
- Dress as if you are going to the gym—meaning, wear sweatpants, hoodie, and cool Nike shoes. Good with very early-stage start-ups.
- Business attire—sometimes business casual really means business attire, which still means wearing a tie and wing tips. Get over it. Good at banks and oil companies.
- Dress like you are meeting Ralph Lauren for lunch—wear the best clothes you have (no polyester) and no tie. Collar turned up.
- Dress like you are a game developer—wear a T-shirt with an old Atari logo, ripped-out jeans, and Converse high tops with no socks.
- Dress like you are not sure of the definition of business casual— khaki pants and a golf shirt are what everyone will wear.

All of the above can be categorized as business casual depending on where you are and who you work with. New York City dress is different from

Silicon Valley dress. Bottom line is to know where you are going and to wear what makes you feel comfortable, whatever that might be. Even in a crowd of "business casuals," what you wear will make you either stand out or blend in. You can make the choice. In the meantime, I will hold onto my khakis but keep the blazer in the trunk of the car, just in case.

For women, business casual is even more difficult. Just remember what Coco Chanel famously said, "Today could be your date with destiny. Dress accordingly."

On Multitasking and Other Sins

Who says teenagers are the only ones who can multitask? Ask anyone who has ever been on a conference call. Sometimes we schedule conference calls when we know there are things, other than the conference calls, to be done.

My personal experiment was a day when my son was home from school sick with a cold. On that day I had back-to-back conference calls, but on that same day I had a drop-dead deadline for a big proposal. While my son was in the room under a mountain of covers, I dutifully dialed in to each conference call and put the phone on mute. Since my son was already in the room, I asked him to listen in on the calls. He was seven years old.

I instructed him to listen to the calls, and anytime my name was called or mentioned, he would holler, "Dad, Dad, they called your name." For this, he was handsomely paid.

Each time my name was called and my son would holler I would interrupt my work on the proposal preparation, get to the phone, and take it off of mute. I would say, "Sorry, I had it on mute. What was that again?"

By the end of the day, I had finished my proposal, my attendance was duly noted on all the conference calls, my young son was talking about activity analysis and cost reductions, and he made twenty bucks. Everyone was happy.

Now that is what I call multitasking.

Nothing Like the Smell of Pot
in the Morning

The currency of venture capitalists is deals. Deals are what VCs see all day, every day. The deals dictate the success or failure of an investor. As an investor, I was preparing for my day with my assistant. Through the dark-tinged glass I spied three young guys in the parking lot. They were going over a PowerPoint presentation and rehearsing to each other, getting ready to meet with any of the hundreds of VCs in the surrounding buildings. I could see them but they couldn't see me.

I commented to my assistant, "Isn't it a little early in the morning to be smoking dope?" It was 9:00 a.m. She agreed, as we returned to trying to figure out my calendar.

My 9:30 appointment was announced and showed up in the conference room to give their pitch and, sure enough, it was the gang of three from the parking lot. The three young entrepreneurs pitched an idea for a video game. During the presentation my assistant kept interrupting to see if we needed anything like Snickers bars or snacks. They were not funded.

It wasn't about the pot. It was a lot about their idea and a lot about their poor judgment.

Are There Awards for Bad Judgment?

Most of us have jobs that can take us to Las Vegas now and again. It is usually for a conference where billions of people, taxi lines, and name tags are involved. Not much fun for most of us, but it is there that poor behavior can emerge from those you least expect it. And that behavior can haunt you. What happens in Las Vegas does not stay in Las Vegas. What happens anywhere does not stay there. Physically or virtually.

It happens in the workplace every day. Those subtle racist jokes circulated through e-mail are not funny. Diversity is not a joke. The nude photos from your old fraternity brothers are in bad taste. The mean homophobic tweets are not amusing or interesting. Most actions like these can get you in trouble.

I am not sure why I have to remind people that such acts are in bad taste, in some cases illegal, and will reflect so poorly on you. If you want to get fired, show a little racism. And you should be.

Keep Those Business Cards

Remember the Rolodex? It was a handy contraption shaped like a Ferris wheel full of cards, and was handy for names and addresses. A Rolodex is a collector's item these days. It has been replaced by the virtual Rolodex of many sorts. A million Rolodex wheels can now fit on your smartphone.

That old wheel had a lot of virtues not to be found in technology. It was easy to use, not driven by a power source, and sort of cool to spin around. Most importantly, the Rolodex gave us somewhere to put all those business cards. It was like a business card display case for all of our relationships.

The tech world creates confusion about business cards. They seem old-fashioned. Do we even need them? Yes. Everyone still carries them and uses them. Being in the work world without a business card is like being in the Wild West without a horse. Don't let anyone tell you otherwise.

Always be ready when the question is raised, "Do you have a card?"

Blind Squirrels and Acorns

Sometimes when technology works we feel lucky. It could be after a big system conversion or when we send an e-mail from the back of a taxi. We depend on the technology and take it for granted, until it doesn't work. When it doesn't work we need to rely on the fifteen-year-old neighbor kid, who is always available or, my favorite person, the IT guy.

Used to be that the IT guy was a nerd who toiled in the bowels of the organization, sometimes literally in the basement. The basement is rarely the case now. More likely, the IT guy is part of the leadership of the organization, as well he or she should be. Without the IT guy, we would be like blind squirrels looking for acorns when it comes to fixing technology.

Keeping Up Is Hard to Do

We all try. We all try to stay current on what is happening in technology. But, wow, it is difficult. What is big data? Where is the cloud? How does Google Maps know where I am? I met a guy the other day who doesn't understand the Internet. He wants to go to Dayton, Ohio, because that is where he thinks it is located. Along with the UFOs. I don't want to be that guy.

But some of the new big ideas are complicated.

Big data is in everything written about privacy and our lives. I always thought data was about the same size. The Internet of Things is now a buzz phrase too. I am hard pressed to name *one thing* that is not on the Internet already. Bitcoin is a really hard one. Near as I can tell, it is virtual money for nonvirtual (or other virtual) things. I am all for that.

In technology, what was once crazy is now normal.

It's hard to stay abreast of everything that is going on at work right now.

If I buy an iPad, can I still buy books?

My boss is asking me to do more work; if I say no will I lose my job?

How long should I wait before I respond to e-mail?

Is someone really following everything I do on the web?

Should I let my coworkers see my Facebook account?

It can make us feel overwhelmed and guilty for what we can't control. But there are some who don't let it get to them.

My friend in the office agreed to go to a seminar on H1N1 so he could orient the entire office about it when he returned.

He told me he was all excited to be picked but then he quietly asked me, "Is H1N1 about immigration or flu shots? Either way, I will learn everything I can," he said.

So however far behind and overwhelmed you might feel, don't worry, there are always those behind you.

Get Me Some of That Inner Work Life

When the people at McKinsey write a report, people listen. Here is one of the latest findings…

In a multiyear research project McKinsey found that, of all the traits and nuances of a job that lead to satisfaction, the single most important is making progress in meaningful work.

Even small wins boost what the researchers call "inner work life." People are more creative, productive, committed, and collegial in their jobs when they have positive inner work lives.

But it's not just any sort of progress in work that matters. The first, and fundamental, requirement is that the work be meaningful to the people doing it.

Unfortunately, the McKinsey people also discovered that most bosses fall into traps that get right in the way of both progress and meaningful work. Aaargh.

All it takes is progress on meaningful work for happy campers? Come on, bosses. We can do better.

Gadgets and Gizmos Galore

I thought I was driving alone but right now there is a woman in my car yelling at me because I just made the wrong turn. I know where I am going but she insists I am wrong. She is the GPS lady.

My cell phone is sending me little beeps reminding me of meetings and buzzing with excitement of the new e-mails I've received.

I am in the process of changing from one laptop computer to another but I don't trust myself to make the conversion so I carry both. It's like they are mating in my black bag.

But when I watch TV today all the commercials make me feel like I am missing out on all the latest cool new stuff. When I hear my tech buddies talk about their cool new devices I feel like a caveman.

Am I getting left behind? Maybe. But I think for now I have more than enough to be productive and do my job. When the flux capacitor comes out, I might reconsider.

The Facebook Thing

I have lots of friends on Facebook; some of them I even know. At a conference recently, one of my "friends" was sitting next to me. I recognized him by his photo and knew that he recently visited Costa Rica and likes Tom Petty and cabernet sauvignon. I could tell by our "friends in common" that I sort of should know him and his world. But what am I supposed to do now that he is sitting right next to me? I like him better as a virtual friend on Facebook, not a guy to have a latte with at a conference. He is glancing at me too.

What is the protocol here? Should I extend my hand and say, "Hey, you are my friend on Facebook"? We both sat there for a minute and then just got up and left, never having said a word to each other.

And what about those friend requests from smiling, skimpily clad people in other countries who I think I don't know? Do I know them from college? Do I know them at all? What if I friend them and my wife views my friends and starts asking questions? How did they even find me? Are they like the exiled Nigerian prince who wants my credit card number? Okay, I will keep them in the waiting to decide category.

And about that Facebook photo? Should it be that "daytime TV soap opera glossy photo" kind? Will people think I am hiding if I don't put my own photo on my page? Should I change the photo now and then? What about those photos of boomers riding Harleys or surfing or skydiving? I don't do any of that. At least I know it is in really bad form to post a question mark where the photo should be. It is FACEbook.

I guess one can never have too many friends. Or maybe you can have too many friends. I just wish they weren't all so happy.

Does Facebook Work at Work?

It was only a matter of time; social networks are now part of the corporate culture. Companies big and small are using social networks as a tool to communicate with employees and customers.

The set of rules, etiquette, and norms for the social networks at work is still developing. The rules about posting at work are different from what you might do at home after a few margaritas. For work postings, there are only two simple rules:

1. Whatever you post, make it about work.
2. Never post anything you don't want your boss to see.

We have all learned from Craigslist, Twitter, Facebook, and all the others that social media can be an incredibly efficient way to both gather and disseminate information. Maybe now, finally, internal communications are more about getting things done than company picnics and employee anniversaries.

No doubt, there will be more than a few embarrassing posts about vacations and children. Social networks are just another part of, well, work. It's a good thing.

More Than an Abbreviation

Three-letter messages are mainstream in the workplace. We have moved from simple FTIs to more refined ones like LOL and TMI. The abbreviations now morph from a text message to headlines of presentations. One that is roaming around in text language really caught my eye. It is "TL;DR." This is a shortcut to an important message: Too Long; Didn't Read. It is a brilliant addition to the language. As opposed to other new clipped responses like WTF, TL;DR is nuanced.

And it captures the tone of the workplace today. We are all running too fast for long memos and reports. What we want is a crisp message, and if there are details, include a few bullets. Anything that is long will end up in the pile of "I will get to it someday." May as well call that the TL:DR stack.

Cancel My Subscription, Please

Everyone receives a lot of e-mails. In fact, for most of us, if we don't have a lot of e-mails clogging up our inbox, we wonder if something might be wrong—like we are about to be fired or have bad breath.

We all figure out quickly which e-mails are important and which ones are not. And we hope our filters take out the annoying ones. But they don't—every day a bunch come through asking me to attend a conference or buy an e-mail list or, for twelve hours only, fly to Fiji.

Most of the annoying mail has a half-hidden note that says: If you no longer wish to receive these e-mails, please reply to this message with "Unsubscribe" in the subject line or simply click on the following link: Unsubscribe.

I pound Unsubscribe all day, and guess what? The exact same e-mails return day after day. It's the unsubscribe conspiracy!

Maybe we all need unsubscribe enforcers.

Three Things E-Mail Is Not

E-mail governs our lives. It has replaced telephone calls, real mail, and water cooler conversations all at once. We complain about the number of e-mails we receive, but if the number of e-mails goes down, we wonder what's wrong.

I like e-mail and, like you, I receive a lot. I like its efficiency but don't confuse e-mail for anything other than the communication tool it is. I know three things that e-mail is not.

First, it is not a list of things to do. Your list of things to do is about doing your job, not draining e-mail.

Second, it is not a gauge of how productive (or popular) you are. If you receive a lot of e-mail, it probably means you send out a lot of e-mail.

Third, it is not a chamber of guilt for all the things you have not done.

Love your e-mail, and you will be more effective.

Am I Ringing?

Lately, I have been having spasms in my upper legs. When it happens I've reached for my cell phone because the sensation is just like the phone ringing in my pocket. It turns out it's a common malady and it is called phantom cell phone vibration syndrome. Ask around, see if you can find someone who believed the smartphone in their pocket was vibrating but found when they checked that there was nothing new. No call. No text.

Research is showing that phantom vibrations is just one of many problems associated with our technology obsession. Research also says we check our cell phones at least every four minutes. We are addicted, admit it. And I am not sure there is any turning back.

The downside to our tech addiction is that it hurts our social relationships. And we all see that everywhere too.

At least now that I know I suffer from phantom cell phone vibrations I can stop worrying about spasms.

Does Cell Phone Etiquette Exist?

I bought a new cell phone recently and the experience was like buying a car. It took hours, and the plans and features were endless. The only option not available was *not* having a cell phone. Our relationship with cell phones is complicated. Is it our friend or enemy?

Studies show that using cell phones makes it harder to multitask, with driving being the best example. A professor went so far as to string money up a tree on low-hanging branches and watch as people on cell phones ducked around the bills.

We have our phones with us most of the time—and for many, that includes in bed. We take our phones to social gatherings, just in case we would rather check e-mail than talk to the guy who boasts about his kids. Who hasn't seen that romantic young couple sitting at a candlelit table, the two of them looking at their phones instead of each other?

Yet that little device in our hands holds the knowledge of the century as well as videos of cats dancing on pianos. It allows for constant communication with loved ones around the world and has an infinite array of other uses. It is the device that changed the world.

And, for all of the beauty of that phone, it is still okay to talk with each other sometimes. You know, the kind of talk that requires using your mouth and ears.

Password Pressure

Change your passwords, everyone tells me each week. I can't. On the list of things we don't want to do, changing passwords is up there with doing taxes and going to the DMV. But change we must in order to avoid what will surely be incessant cyber attacks. Passwords are becoming a bigger and bigger part of our lives. For a guy who couldn't remember his high school locker combination, this is a problem. For all the security benefits, passwords for everything we do can be a real hassle.

It is almost impossible now to use the same password in all situations. Some passwords are case sensitive, some need to be long, some need to include numbers, and some need to include a smiley face. For me, all are easy to forget.

And now the prompts to help you remember your password are even more difficult. No longer do they ask for your mother's maiden name, now they want to know the name of your first-grade teacher's cat. Gone are the days of a pet's name or 123456.

I used to be cavalier about passwords but I now have password religion based on one bad experience. All the recent attacks we hear about make it clear that hackers are spending more time trying to crack into our cyber lives and there are lots of places to get tech help on this. If the entire world is always changing passwords, someday we might run out of password options. Now password police are requiring symbols like hash marks and ampersands.

So, for those of you who list all your passwords on the yellow sticky on your monitor, it might be time for some new password ideas. In our work lives there are many activities that we look forward to and that give us great satisfaction. And then there are those other activities that can ruin a day.

I Forgot My Computer!

It was dark when I had to leave the house for a day full of meetings. I loaded up my big black bag in the darkness with all the power cords, notebooks, and paraphernalia that make for a productive workday.

When I arrived at the office I realized I had packed everything *except* my computer. What should I do? It was too late to go home to get it. I felt like I was naked in a world of fashionistas. I felt like I was without a weapon in a war. I calmed down and reconciled myself to a day without my PC.

And guess what, it was the most productive day I've had in a long time.

I could think without constant distractions. I could plan and set priorities. I could talk to people and listen. I got away from my desk and met the new guy down the hall. It was like a day way back in the '90s.

Now I'm thinking about forgetting my computer every once in a while.

That Google Doodle Is Smart

Google is a big part of our lives. We see the Google logo every day when we click on dancing cats or calculus tutorials. Most days, when the Google logo is converted into a doodle, the animations are entertaining and catch our attention.

When the Google Doodle popped up on my birthday, I was surprised. The doodle was all decked out in birthday candles. Wow, I thought, someone famous must have the same birthday as me. Who could it be? What a coincidence.

But it wasn't a greeting for everyone, it was just for me. How did Google know? Wait? How *did* they know?

By now, we know that each time we click, travel, charge something to a credit card, use a cell phone, use GPS, tweet, friend someone, rent a movie, make a dinner reservation, or breathe the data is captured. My birthday is a part of big data.

I still like the Google Doodle. I just wish it wasn't so smart. What else does Google know?

The WTF Thing

A boss I had early in my career was not one prone to long missives or helpful critiques. I would send him reports and analyses and he would send back notes with three letters on them. The three letters were WTF.

I knew his short responses were because he was so busy that he couldn't even spell it out. I assumed the responses were really questions, like, "What's this for?" or "Will this fly?" or "Why the face?" Or, I thought he might be in meetings at the World Trade Federation and he was sending me some kind of shorthand about that, since he might not want others to know. I learned that WTF is sort of a question and sort of a statement that requires an exclamation point.

WTF is a sentiment that can capture both being puzzled and frustrated at the same time and can come in handy at work.

About Those Tattoos

Imagine biking to a job interview through the swamp-like humidity of Portland in the summertime. You're wearing a vegan T-shirt that fits you more tightly than it should, thanks to your alterations (cutting up the seam, removing fabric, re-sewing). Across your chest, you're sporting a sling backpack fashioned from an old canvas drop cloth. Your feet are showing through holes in your shoes. Your beard is unruly, your hair unwashed. Your neck tattoos are slathered in sweat. You walk into the interview.

The hiring managers regard you like you're manna from heaven. You get the job.

This happened to a friend of mine, whom I'll call Ian. Ian usually picks up painting/drawing/design gigs online, but decided to interview for a "real job" illustrating medical pamphlets.

He claims he got the job because his image was consistent with what the company expected of a twenty-first-century artist—earthy, DIY, nonconformist. From what I heard, the ten-minute interview following his entrance was irrelevant, conducted as a formality.

When you're hiring for a position (in this case, illustrator) that's so completely outside your normal realm (in this case, health care), I'm sure it's hard not to be impressionable. Maybe you don't even know what practical criteria to use. But what if you knew that Ian arrived sweaty and dressed down for that very reason? That he *knew* he gave off an artist's aura and thus nixed the button-down? That his free-spirited look was actually *calculated*?

Not changing out of hipster attire is indeed as much a choice as saying, "I need to iron creases into my best linen slacks." In my opinion, whatever is worn to an interview is calculated, no matter the industry or end result. Nowadays, candidates are just trying to stand out from the crowd, and "looking the part" is the in-person equivalent of innovating your resume or having a relevant social media presence. Dressing to reflect your industry certainly makes you more memorable than wearing generic business attire. But the advantages may be hit or miss.

Apparently, image profiling runs rampant.[1] Upstart tech companies feel that a candidate is missing a key component if he or she isn't sporting a local band tee or discussing the fine distinctions between obscure microbrews.

Now, you *could* lump all of this under the guise of hiring for culture. But I'm sure you've all been surprised by a candidate whose image "conflicted" with his or her skills or personality ... right?

I Want My Cubicle!

The reports are in—open-space work environments are not all they are cracked up to be. To anyone who sits in the middle of the floor surrounded by coworkers this is *not* news.

Sure, open spaces cut down on the sense of hierarchy and break down all those closed doors, but there are unintended consequences. All those stray conversations kill concentration and there are NO secrets. Distractions abound. So lots of people are complaining, especially the non-millennial workers who are not used to this environment.

The solution? Everyone wears headphones and people prop up posters and plants to create separation. And that's why so many are out in hallways or in the bathroom on their cell phone. As always, a one-size work space does not fit all.

Greater openness at work is here to stay, but sometimes we just want to go cocoon somewhere. Even if it's our old cubicle.

Apple Store Anxiety

Let me say first that I love Apple products. My mind works like an Apple product works, with intuition and common sense. I have a bunch of Apple products.

The problem is, to buy an Apple product or to repair an Apple product, one has to go into an Apple Store. Call me a heretic, but I would rather go to the dentist. At least at the dentist, there is no line.

When I enter the Apple Store it's like a college party where everyone knows everyone else. And I don't know anyone. Recently, my beloved laptop needed a repair and I desperately needed the computer. I was told with a smile that I could have an appointment in a week. I can't wait a week, but for now my smartphone will have to do.

Leaving an Apple Store is like leaving the DMV: I waited, nothing is fixed, and I know I will have to come back. At least the Apple Store has happier people.

Pluto Is the New Benchmark

Space junkies and geeks are jubilant. Incredibly, to me at least, NASA launched a spacecraft, *New Horizons*, that landed on Pluto. Okay, it didn't *land* on Pluto, but it sure came close.

But it reminds me to ponder tech questions closer to home.

The NASA spacecraft travels at 31,000 miles per hour. Why does it take so long to get an appointment at an Apple Store?

The spacecraft is sending thousands of high-resolution photos from three billion miles away. Why doesn't my printer work? It's right next to my computer.

Since there are no electric outlets in space, there must be a very cool power source. Why does my laptop keep running out of power?

What NASA has done for discovery and innovation is incredible.

Now, when I talk to our IT people, Pluto is the new comparison. If they can do that, why can't we do this?

Oh, That Sinking Feeling

It is one of *those* things. It's like the split second between when you stub your toe and when it hurts like a bastard. With this thing, as soon as you do it, you know you made a mistake that is irretrievable. I am talking about sending an e-mail to the wrong people.

We have all done it, and there are few feelings that are worse. When I inadvertently copied an e-mail to the people who I least wanted to see the message, it took me weeks to recover through apologizing and promises to do better. The "cc" line can be a dangerous thing.

The REPLY ALL and the SEND buttons combined can be more dangerous to a career than showing up drunk at the holiday party.

Once the damaging message is sent, it is gone, gone, gone. A follow-up that says, "Please ignore," or any attempt to retrieve it, only makes the reader more interested. The damage is done.

Next time you write that controversial or inflammatory e-mail, take another look at the cc's and the bcc's before you hit the send button. You will thank me.

A Wealth of Webinars

I like webinars okay. Some are better than others. Webinars are a good way to stay abreast of industry and tech changes and hear a good sales pitch at the same time. More likely, a webinar is a good way to try to learn about one thing while you are doing something else on your computer.

Yikes, there are a lot of webinars, which makes me wonder, how many do we really need? In one day I was invited to webinars on B-to-B sales generation, compensation trends, and making the most of connections. Then there were the webinars on ERP, OCD, and SAP, all for my FYI and all for free. I am suspicious of free webinars. Free webinar sounds like another way to say, "I want you to buy something from me."

Free or not, if a webinar can make us more productive and successful, let's attend. It's just impossible to figure out which one will do that.

The one webinar I might attend is: How to choose which webinar to attend.

Dancing with Office Chairs

Fancy office chairs are as much a part of the workplace as backpacks and headphones. Anytime people start settling into a conference room for a meeting, the first ten minutes are spent trying to figure out how to adjust the chair.

Under each seat there are an array of knobs and levers and gauges that are supposed to make us more comfortable. We would adjust the height, the back, the arms, and the angle of the dangle if we could only figure out how the chair works.

Often, once it is determined that no one knows how to adjust the chairs, everyone glances around to swap chairs. The result is musical office chairs with attempts at more adjustments. The big guy usually ends up on the floor after being a little too aggressive on the recline button.

Sometimes the chair that looks like a dog chewed on the arms and that has no adjustment options is the most comfortable. Sometimes sitting in a chair with no adjustments, distractions, or bells and whistles also makes for the most productive meeting. Overengineering is overrated.

Tech, Tech, Tech, and More Tech

Not long ago I beamed with pride when I figured out how the copy machine works. I was the master of all things double sided. But my technology challenges are only escalating. While commuting, I am really driving a computer; a car came with it. I will never understand the permutations and combinations of options on the dashboard.

Now the office has a new coffee machine. It presents a set of options that I cannot deal with early in the morning. Do I want an espresso, a latte, or a cappuccino? I cannot find the button for plain old coffee. I want a button that says, just make the decision for me and make it snappy. By next year, I expect the coffee machine to prepare my tax returns.

Technology is all about making us happier at work. Sometimes, I am so happy I can hardly stand it.

Another Technology List

Innovation is everywhere. Everyone is talking about it. So much so that it is difficult to keep track of all the new tools that are making our lives easier. Based on a nonscientific poll, here are some innovations that have truly changed the workplace and our business lives.

1. **The mute button**—creates silence when you need it most.
2. **Texting**—don't feel like talking? No problem. Also helped create a new shorthand language. The ultimate efficiency tool.
3. **Yellow stickies**—to the office, what duct tape is to the rest of the applied world.
4. **Wheelies**—the back-saving device that turned all luggage rectangular and too big to fit under the seat in front of you. Why did it take so long?
5. **Virtuality**—allows one to be anywhere and work, or not.

We can all agree, how did we live without wheelies?

High on Whiteboard Markers
and Presentations

Whiteboards are as much a part of the workplace as chairs that are too complicated to adjust. Whiteboards are in conference rooms, kitchens, and cubicles. And, there are those people who *always* seem to be at the whiteboard pontificating and doodling at the same time. No matter the place, I have noticed whiteboard rituals that are universal.

The first is that whiteboards are impossible to erase. No matter how hard you push and slide, remnants of past meetings remain.

I notice, too, that there are never good markers. They are always dry and worn out. When you do find a good one, the fumes from whiteboard markers can induce an entire conference room into a coma.

And the more one needs to use the whiteboard, the more likely it is that a Do Not Erase sign will be on it. Upon inspection, these whiteboards always have an impressive but indecipherable code on them. Some are adorned with complicated formulas full of sigma and pi symbols. The equations could solve the mystery of the universe but I think they are put there just to look smart.

A lot of whiteboards feature words like "strategic" and "priorities" followed by a list. The list always includes words like "communications," "mission," and "stakeholders." Those whiteboards seem to never get erased and no one pays attention to them.

Every whiteboard features artwork way down by the tray that holds the erasers. It is primitive but happy art. The art was created by all the bored kids who entertained themselves while Mom or Dad tried to get something done, usually on a weekend. The art kid's artwork is more unique than whatever Mom or Dad was doing.

Whiteboards are good reminders that sometimes things need to be erased and we need to start all over. Don't let a whiteboard be a daily reminder of regrets or a source of guilt for what is not complete.

So be thankful for that clean whiteboard with new markers and just ignore the fumes. In the world of whiteboards, little things count.

What's Your Walk-Up Song?

Every major league baseball player has a "walk-up song." It's the anthem played in the stadium as the player is walking from the on-deck circle and getting ready to bat. It creates the swagger, the identity for the player. Is he a hip-hop guy? A classic rock guy? A weird song guy? In all cases, the song is supposed to get the player psyched to hit a 96-mph fastball and the crowd amped up for a big at bat. Woo-hoo. Ballplayers now list their walk-up song next to their batting average and RBIs.

Sometimes a song becomes inseparable from the player. Think "Wild Thing" for Charlie Sheen in the movie *Major League*. Or, the Metallica song "Enter Sandman," which meant Yankees closer Mariano Rivera was entering the game. Head for the hills! What does this have to do with the workplace?

Before a recent speaking engagement I was asked to name my own walk-up song. And it made sense. Every day, we are walking from the on-deck circle into a meeting or a presentation or something that requires a little high voltage. We all need a walk-up song, but it is not as easy to pick as it might seem at first glance. Is my walk-up song Aaron Copland's "Fanfare for the Common Man"? It would show a thoughtful and inclusive side. Or is it "Back in Black" by AC/DC? That song would show I am all about implementation. Either can get me fired up to face the work world.

More importantly, now I know, we should all have a walk-up song, at least one that we play in our head when we are approaching the batter's box. We especially need it on Monday mornings. It's that tune that helps us think we are going to hit a home run every time.

Are Sports Metaphors Dead?

We have all been to business meetings that are more like pep rallies. It's almost always a situation where we are being asked to try harder or to do more with less. We might hear things like:

This is a third and ten situation.

Or, with this plan we are "throwing a Hail Mary," or even combinations like "this won't be a layup so we need to keep our eye on the ball."

Today, sports metaphors are way out of favor. They may not work because lots of people are not sports fans and, in a global economy, not all sports are understood by all. Instead, we need to use more generic metaphors to get our message across.

The problem is that sports metaphors are ingrained in the workplace and finding others is not a slam dunk. So while you try to hit it out of the park with new non-sports metaphors, remember we are still in the early innings.

Presentation Poisons

We've all been there, standing up in front of the room, lights dimmed, projector whirring, and the PowerPoint shining brightly on the screen. People are paying attention and taking notes. It's all good, and we are starting to feel confident and smooth. We are thinking maybe there's even a raise in our future if things continue to go so well. Then one of the attendees raises a hand and asks, "Can I ask a question?"

Uh-oh, we think, and say, "Sure." But we know our rhythm is already broken. Then the comment comes and the air is sucked out of the room. Disaster strikes. We know the presentation may as well be over.

Any number of comments and phrases can derail a presentation. Phrases like, "We need more data" or "We need to change the agenda" or "Sorry to cut you short" are among them. Even a request for a bathroom break can be an act from which a presentation never recovers. But there are three phrases that are surefire presentation killers. Here they are:

1. **Those numbers don't look right.** This phrase is almost always uttered by the most senior person in the room or the most analytical person who really does understand the numbers. And the chances are, that person is right, and the number is wrong. There is no recovery except to say that we will double check the numbers and get back to you. But the presentation is over because after the questions about that page, nothing else is believable.

2. **Can we do a process check?** When this question is raised it means no one knows what the hell we are talking about anymore. The discussion has gone so far off track that people started checking e-mail long ago. "Process check" is another way to ask what subject we are on. When the question comes up, it means you have let the conversation go too far afield from the reason anyone showed up for the meeting in the first place.

3. **I know you can't read this, but...** We have all heard the phrase and there is always a collective sigh of resignation in the room when we hear it. Anyone who hears this phrase takes it as permission to do something else

during the presentation. A synonym for this phrase alludes to an eye chart. Why pay attention to something you can't read? Never, ever show anything that no one can read.

The remedy for all three phrases is simple. Prepare. Prepare. Prepare.

Make sure all the numbers are right. Don't let the meeting go off track. Be a leader and show pictures, not data that no one can read. Presentation skills can make or break a career.

The Praying at Work Thing

It wasn't my meeting, but when I walked by the conference room I saw the PowerPoint presentation up on the screen and I saw the person up front talking and using a laser pointer. She was into it.

But to my surprise, those sitting around the table were all praying. Their heads were bowed and their hands were clasped in their laps in solemn silence. That's unusual, I thought. When I looked closer, I saw that everyone in the room except the presenter was staring down at his iPhone or BlackBerry!

They were doing e-mail or texting and not paying any attention at all. What a productive meeting.

If we want people to pay attention at work, it might be time to have people leave their smartphones at the door like they did with six-shooters in the old days.

And say a prayer that people won't be praying during your next presentation.

The R Word and the B Word

People at work are complaining about the overuse of the R word. Really? Yes, that's the word—"really." As in, your colleague asks you for help and your snarky response is, "Really?" Or when you see what your lunch mate is eating and you raise your eyebrows and say, "Really?"

As much as the word "really" is overused, the killer word at work is really the B word. No, not that one. The word is BUT.

B-U-T. As in, I could have finished the project on time, but I had a flat tire. Or, I like working here BUT. Or, I hate my job and don't perform BUT. Or, this could have been a better radio piece BUT.

Want to be better at work and like your job? Stop using BUT. Really.

Where Is the Elevator?

The term "elevator speech" seems to be all the rage, especially in Silicon Valley. Funny, because I don't think most of the buildings in Silicon Valley have elevators.

Anyway, an elevator speech is that crisp and tantalizing description one can give to a potential investor or employer in the time it takes to get from the lobby to their appointed floor.

Most times I am on an elevator, no one talks to anyone else. Even if anyone did talk, I don't think the rest of the occupants would want to hear a pitch.

I know, it's just a metaphor to emphasize how important it is to have a short, compelling message. But wait, I am all for that.

In fact, I think poor communication skills are the one thing that hurts people's careers more than anything else. Knowing the key message that you want to convey is more important than all the fluff around it. I like the elevator speech for Virgin America—"We fly airplanes."

Come to think of it, maybe we need more elevators so we can communicate better.

Eating in Your Car

I see you out there. Sitting in your car on your way to work. Stuck in traffic. Thinking about your boss. Probably running late. Probably have to go the bathroom but there is nowhere to stop. Without a headset, you can't talk on your cell phone and you don't dare send out any text messages. What's left? I know what you're thinking—I will eat in the car.

Danger! Danger!

There might be health risks to eating in the car. There certainly are driving risks. But the biggest risk is that you are going to spill that meal all over yourself and further ruin your day.

I know you will continue to have that latte while driving. But in the spirit of making your day easier, here is the list of three foods to absolutely avoid while driving:

1. Burrito—they always unravel into your lap
2. Whoppers and Big Macs—that special sauce is a killer
3. Leftovers—if you need a fork, don't try it

Certain foods are so obvious that I won't insult your judgment. Think jelly doughnuts.

You can do it! Eat once you get to the office.

Redundant Conversations Again

Instant recognition hits like a lightbulb clicking on with the phrase "redundant conversations." We know exactly what the phrase means, and we don't like it. The phrase instills irritation and a series of questions like:

- Haven't we covered this before?
- Why are we talking about this again?
- Why are we wasting time on this?

And the worst question of all about redundant conversations is: Won't someone *please* make a decision?

Redundant conversations are too often a part of the organization's culture. These conversations can create lots of DO OVERS and wasted time. I know one company where the problem is so prevalent that the CEO's space is called The Office of Redundancy Office. What a waste. We are all too busy to suffer from too much talk and not enough decision making.

If you are trapped in the web of redundant conversations, it's best to change the subject. Maybe then someone will finally make a decision.

All Aboard

At one time it was called new employee orientation. Before that it was called getting thrown into the deep end of the pool to see if you can swim.

Today, starting a new job is called onboarding.

Onboarding is the process whereby new people are effectively transitioned into the organization. If it is done well.

Starting a new job is like an initiation without the hazing. It can be painful. Onboarding is designed to eliminate that pain. Onboarding takes care of all the things that can be frustrating when starting a job. It's hard to be productive when you don't know the simple things like the locations of the bathrooms.

So if you are starting a new job, pay attention during onboarding. Being able to say, "I am the new person," doesn't last for long in today's organizations.

And when it comes to probationary periods, they don't end. We are all on probation every day.

Even Lunch Is a Quandary Wrapped in a Dilemma

To lunch or not to lunch, that is the question.

On one hand, everyone tells me that success is all about developing relationships. And the best time and place to do that is at lunch. Get in touch with those people who can advance your career and work them! No matter where you go at lunch, relationships are developing all around the place.

On the other hand, there is lots of comfort in having a turkey sandwich at your desk. You can get work done, the sodas are probably free, you don't have to get dressed up, and there is much less stress involved in meeting strangers.

Who knew lunch could be so complicated. My advice? Like everything else, find the balance between those $20 chicken Caesars at the restaurant and those dry turkey sandwiches at the desk.

But if your boss invites you out, it's always good to go.

The Thing About Skinny Suits

I know what happened. The guy may have been shopping at Banana Republic or J.Crew with his children so he bought a skinny suit. They look good on the mannequins and the sales help, so why not? The words judgment and discretion leap to mind. The skinny suit didn't work.

Skinny suits are cut for twenty-two-year-olds who are in good shape. The jackets are tight and the pants are tighter. For the not-so-slim guy who is working as a new manager? Not so much. Fashion is important but comfort in clothes and feeling comfortable in one's skin trump fashion every time.

The rules about business attire continue to change. What to wear depends on geography, size of the organization, age of the organization, age of the people who work there, the weather, and just about any other variable one can imagine.

There is no easy way to find rules about what to wear in the changing workplace. The most basic rule is to wear clothes that are age appropriate and that fit.

Cars and Your Work Persona

Face it, your car is a part of your work life. You commute in it, you do conference calls in it, you plan your day in it. The car can impact your career life, whether you know it or not.

I know a venture capitalist who only invests in entrepreneurs who drive fast cars. The VC believes that there is likely to be more action and a little edge in someone who avoids driving a Prius.

If you drive an old beater, the car may send out a message that you need a raise. Or, it may send out a message that you are a slob.

If you drive a Ferrari on a manager's salary, you may send out a message that you don't really need a job. Or, that you are extorting money from the company. Or, that you are a former NBA star.

Next time you go car shopping, think about what your car might say about you. It's now a piece of your wardrobe. Others are watching.

Welcome to Abilene

In the world of group dynamics there is a notion called the Abilene paradox. The story goes that a bunch of people were hanging around in the sweltering heat of Texas, saying, "What do you want to do?" The response was, "I don't know, what do you want to do?" and it went around in a circle like that until everyone agreed they would drive to Abilene, although no one really wanted to do that.

The Abilene paradox is in play when a group agrees to do something that no one wants to do.

Too often, people sit around conference rooms at work and, yes, succumb to the Abilene paradox and agree to do what no one wants to do. Those decisions can really come back to haunt you when you are held accountable.

It is always better to say, "I don't want to do that," than to end up in Abilene.

Do Assholes Always Win?

According to most studies, Americans work an average of forty-seven hours per week, including the time they spent commuting to and from work. The studies found that workers in some cities—like New York and San Francisco—put in more hours than the average American. Nothing could be worse than spending all of that time working for or around an asshole.

An asshole is like pornography: hard to define, but we know one when we see one. In general, an asshole is a bully. An asshole manages through intimidation and fear, and is prone to outbursts at the expense of others. We all know one. If you don't know one, you might be one.

When suffering under an asshole, one might quietly say, "What goes around comes around." Or, "Someday he will get his…" And, in my experience, most do. Don't give up—it may take some time. Assholes do not always win, they lose, and if you work for one, the best way to get even is to get the hell out of there. Since everyone around the jerk will probably make a run for the door, others will notice and the asshole will get what he deserves. I cannot prove this is the case 100 percent of the time, but, yes, they will get what they deserve.

Think of all the hours you put in. Life is too short to suffer working for a jerk. Make the move or, if you can't, start documenting the behavior and get your colleagues to help. Evidence will come in handy; think videos. Do assholes always win? No, but there are exceptions.

The Asshole Hall of Fame

The list is long but not to be named here. We can all name a few from our own experience or folklore, and it is a long list. The hall of fame inductees don't need to be named here because we see them in action every day. Each week, politicians drop out of the race based on documented bad behavior. Every day, a C-level executive is indicted for illegal actions. Professional athletes are suspended for hitting girlfriends or using illegal substances. The well never runs dry. There is a lesson in their journeys that applies to the workplace. The lesson is that careers are ruined, not built, through bad behavior.

The good guys and women still win. Leaders who are authentic, credible, and honest are still the ones who prevail. Show me a good leader, and the word asshole will not be a descriptor.

I would guess that anytime an executive is indicted, others run through the memory banks reflecting on past behaviors at trade shows or the company holiday party. It is hard to live like that.

So next time, before you fudge on the expense report or go into the behavior danger zone, remember that people do get caught—don't get inducted into the asshole hall of fame.

Being Nice at Work

Contrary to what one would think, the number of mean bosses is increasing. In fact, incivility between workers is epidemic. For some of you, this is not a surprise, as you deal with jerks all around you every day. (Note: this fact does not give you the license to become a jerk.)

We all prefer to be around reasonable and nice people, so why is this happening? The research shows that many are skeptical of the returns of being nice. No ROI means no nice people? Studies show that if we are nice we believe we are less leader-like. Even more people believe they will be taken advantage of if they are nice. Wimps don't win.

Yet, the research also shows that we are more productive when we enjoy our coworkers. Organizations are less successful when there is an air of toxicity.

Incivility often grows out of ignorance, not malice. People who are acting like jerks may not know it and will change when confronted with the truth. Maybe there is hope that the jerks will disappear. Buck the trend. Be nice, and you will be more productive and, goshdarnit, people will like you.

The Three Best Bosses You Will Ever Have

Most people can name the best boss and the worst boss they have experienced at work. It's too easy to talk about the worst boss, there are lists and comedy routines about them that are aired every day. Let's explore the good bosses; in fact, let's explore the bosses we love—they are less easy to pin down. There are only three best bosses:

1. **The boss who held you to a higher standard.** This is the boss who said, "It's not good enough." This is the boss who helped you get that promotion and made you better.
2. **The boss who gave you a chance.** This is the boss who threw you into the deep end of the pool because this boss knew you could swim before you knew it. This is the boss who made you realize you can do a lot more than you thought.
3. **The boss who taught you how to be a boss.** This is the boss we want to be someday.

Bosses will come in and out of our careers. The good ones are like the teachers one never forgets. Aspire to be the best boss in someone's career.

Management Gurus?

Management gurus worthy of recognition are all around us. The behavior of the gurus reminds us of what works and what doesn't in today's complex organizations. New managers, especially, take note as some of the gurus show their spots as they run for office or play characters in movies and on TV. Here are just a few of the teachings I have seen from gurus who are unwittingly showing us how to be better managers:

- Listen to others and then dismiss any input. If others were as smart as you, one of them would have your job.
- Know that no matter what is happening, it's always all about you. Without you, the organization would be that much less.
- Form a little clique with the "guys." Make sure others are excluded. A good posse is a manager's best friend.
- Build a personal brand and make it unique. If the brand includes styles that are thirty years out of date, that's everyone else's problem. The style may just come back.
- Petulance matters as much as confidence. If you don't get your way or things are not going like you would like, tantrums may be the answer.
- Take advantage of your power position, including sleeping with anyone in a lesser position.
- Assume that you will never get fired, that you are irreplaceable. And if you do get fired, they will want you back.
- Be bold in all you do, even if you are not sure what you are doing. As the boss, it's important to constantly make big, dramatic decisions.
- Don't worry about keeping up with technology; it will bend to suit you.
- Say and do anything you want while off-line. No one will ever know or find out.

We all owe a debt of gratitude to the gurus for these insights. We learn from all ends of the guru spectrum.

The Corporate Culture Thing

Culture counts, and now there is proof. Merriam-Webster has noted a significant increase in lookups of the word "culture" on the dictionary's website, along with spikes of concentrated interest. Who can argue with a dictionary company? Of all the billions and billions of words in the dictionary, culture is the one with the biggest increases in lookups? I think people are trying to understand the word culture, how to measure it, and, most importantly, how to change it.

I doubt that people were searching for the word because they wanted to qualify as a classical music lover or learn how to eat caviar with the proper spoon. Could be that some are interested in how a pearl develops in an oyster, but I doubt it. There is some probability that interest in culture spiked when yogurt became a major food group. When people looked up culture they were trying to understand what the word means relative to their own organizations. As in, what is corporate culture? What does it look like here? And, do I like the culture here?

I am not surprised that culture is such a popular word. Whether it's a Fortune 500 company, a start-up, a football team, a police force, or a college, the organization's culture dictates all behaviors. Current events are demanding that we look at the organization's culture in a critical way. The culture dictates the answers to the big questions, like:

- What is important and how do we do things around here?
- Who makes decisions and what factors are decisions based on?
- How do we treat each other? With care and respect? Or, everyone is competing and we are all enemies?
- Do we work like dogs or do we bring our dogs to the office?
- Can we really tell the truth to each other?
- Does my contribution count?

When the culture is off track, nothing is quite right. Pay and benefits could be good, maybe you just received a promotion; no matter, you still don't want to go to work in the morning.

We have all been in successful organizations where the culture is not right. (See rowers on Viking ships.) And we have all been in organizations where everyone talks about culture and there are efforts to improve the culture but it still sucks. (See company picnics.) I have heard some say, "My company doesn't have a culture." Yes, it does. When I hear that statement, to me it means you don't like the culture.

Cultures are tough to change. Lots of change efforts have begun with free food and fewer meetings. That approach leads to weight gain but not much change. Some would say the only way to change a culture is to change the people. People changes usually happen after the efforts that involve free doughnuts and employee surveys don't go anywhere.

The fact that so many organizations are looking at culture and that it is the big word for the year is a good thing. And organizations are not just reviewing culture—changes are being made. It's a good idea, and you should be a part of creating that positive culture.

On Powerful Women

Fortune magazine names the "50 Most Powerful Women in Business" each year. And each year it is an impressive bunch that grows in strength and prestige.

Women now run big companies and are doing it well.

Has anything changed? As I listen to the pundits and the *Fortune* reporters discussing what's changed about the progress women have made in the workplace, one theme comes up consistently. The theme is this: women today do not have to act like men to succeed. In short, women can be themselves, with no apologies or change required.

Instead of trying to join the good ol' boys club, successful women today can be, well, women, and all that means.

It's a good thing, and is a big change worth noting for both men and women.

My only question is, what took so long? Be a man, be a woman.

What's an Office?

It can get a little confusing. Friends tell me they are going to the office and hours later I see them in the local Starbucks, sitting at a table working on a laptop.

One of my colleagues claims his office is in the trunk of his car. Millions of people work from their kitchen table—an office can be right next to the pots and pans. I know others who are most productive on airplanes or on their commute.

At most start-ups, an office is a conference table with lots of people sitting around wearing headphones.

The good news is that it doesn't matter. In the workplace today, an office is a state of mind enhanced with technology that allows us to network with the team. And the rest of the team is defining their own office too.

Showing up is not a skill. As long as the work is done, an office can be anywhere.

Can You Hear Me Now?

Any guru or self-help book will broadcast the secrets to being a great leader and, ultimately, career success. The usual list includes determination, a goal-driven orientation, innovation, and passion. It's a good list, and all are worthy of any leader.

But there is another trait, often overlooked, that makes for a great leader. The one trait that is often omitted is: being a good listener. Listening is an underrated skill. People around you take note if you are a good listener or not. If you listen, you might actually learn something. If you listen, you might make better decisions.

When you hear the phrase, "He/she always thinks he/she is the smartest person in the room," that is the sign of a person with a poor listening reputation.

Show me a good manager and I will show you a good listener. You are listening now. Keep working on the skill and you will be heard more.

Watch Out for Fibbing

Fibbing has taken over the work world. Millions of little white lies bounce around cubicles and office spaces every day. No, I am not talking about Enron or any kind of fraud. I am talking about fibs that make you less successful.

Here are a few test questions:

- Do you have a few handy blank taxi receipts around for those expense reports?
- Have you ever been on a project team that was a total disaster but you told everyone the team was on time and on budget?
- Have you ever tried to sell something for the company that you knew was a piece of junk but you didn't say anything?
- Have you ever put a few "extra" words in your resume?

These are just a few examples of the fibs that can catch up to you. And you don't need to see an employee manual or business book.

Instead, just recall stories like "Pinocchio," "The Emperor's New Clothes," and "The Boy Who Cried Wolf."

What's Important?

How to separate the Urgent from the Critical from the Very Important from REQUIRES IMMEDIATE ATTENTION!

I receive more than a few e-mails every day with that bright red exclamation point prominently displayed. These notes all seem important and imply that an immediate response is required. And I always do read them immediately. Then there are those notes, invites, and messages that include words like urgent, critical, or the dreaded ASAP in the title line. The messages are hot and always get the most of my attention too. They imply that someone's hair is on fire or nuclear holocaust is impending. There are a lot of them.

THEN THERE ARE THOSE NOTES IN ALL CAPS AND USUALLY IN THE COLOR RED. IT IS A TRICK TO DOUBLE ENSURE OUR ATTENTION IS SNAGGED. THE MESSAGE COULD BE FROM A NIGERIAN PRINCE, THE BOSS, A BILL COLLECTOR, OR THE FIRE DEPARTMENT. WE HAVE TO READ THEM.

What are we supposed to do? How do we decipher what's important with this constant barrage of imperatives? Is what the boss wants always the most important? What about the customer? What about the team? What about my blood pressure? It's almost like a workplace contest to see who can cause the most stress with emergencies.

The options to deal with this constant sense of urgency may be simple. Here is a sample of how to deal with the urgency barrage:

1. **Rely on your judgment.** The most important decision we make every day is deciding what's important. And only you know what is truly important. Who knows better than you how your contribution will make the organization more successful? Make the decision about what is important or others will make it for you—and you may not like what they decide. What is important could be the accumulation of many small significant activities. Waiting for something that is earth-shatteringly important is to wait for something that may never happen.

2. **Develop your own sorting system.** Like sorting grades of eggs, we all need to sort the source of the urgent messages we receive. The boss is probably going to be sorted near the top of the stack. Anything from the family marked urgent will be ahead of the boss. Anything from an airline regarding your flight will be way up there. Then, there are all the others that need to be sorted. Remember, what is critical to others might or might not be critical to you. The chronic offender, like Chicken Little, should probably be ignored.

3. **Don't be fooled and distracted.** Then there are those messages, sometimes from friends, that rage, "Stop everything you are doing to watch this." What do we do? We stop everything to watch what is usually the latest cool YouTube video. We laugh, we enjoy it, we probably pass it on, but is it urgent and does it require a work stoppage? No. Don't get faked out by the faux urgent.

It is now to the point that I appreciate it when someone tells me, you don't need to read this right now—it is not that important. Or the important thing you need to know is in paragraph three. Or, this is not urgent, deal with it when you can. Maybe it's time for all of us to take a deep breath when it comes to urgency, develop our own measured system in what we send and receive, and remember that the most important message is not at the top of the incoming mail from someone who guarantees you a job for $75 an hour at Amazon.

I can tell you one thing—when it comes to importance, checking social media sites first thing every day or, worse, all the time, is not in the top three on the urgency scale.

Is That Day Really Necessary?

National Boss Day is now an annual event. Awkward. I am never sure about the proper protocol. Should I bring my boss a box of chocolates? Will the boss think I am sucking up to him? Or, if I don't bring the chocolates, will I pay for it next time I am up for a raise?

Why do we need this holiday, I ask you. Any boss knows who's the boss and acts that way. Most bosses probably dread the holiday too. They probably try to play hooky on that day so they don't have to deal with it.

The guy at Hallmark who invented this holiday must be the boss. Or maybe the day was created in response to National Executive Assistant Day.

I don't even like the word boss. Sounds like somebody who would yell.

But the holiday rolls around each year with fanfare—National Boss Day. I plan to pay homage each year—by ignoring it.

I Have a Suggestion

Once upon a time, there were suggestion boxes all over every place in the world. The corporate office, the hotel lobby, the YMCA, everywhere. They were usually wooden boxes with a slot on top and a little lock on the side. Maybe there was an envelope taped to the side filled with three-by-five cards to capture that brilliant suggestion.

Sometimes the box would include constructive feedback that someone could use. Often, the suggestions were about where the boss could shove his ideas. More likely, a peek into the box would show that it was full of gum wrappers and used tea bags.

We still have suggestion boxes, but now the box doesn't hang on the wall. The new suggestion box has lots of names, including employee surveys and all the anonymous message boards and websites that evaluate everything. Everyone can comment about everything. Some of the feedback I see in these electronic places is about as useful as the gum wrappers. It is too easy to be snarky and critical when you know others will see your comments but not know who you are.

Here is my suggestion: try to be helpful to others. Try to make the place better with any comments and suggestions you might make. Come up with your own ideas before you jump on others'.

THE Worst Boss Announcement

We have all heard the boss say something that made us scratch our head and wonder if there was a hidden meaning to the words. But, among all utterances, there is one statement that we really do not want to hear:

"Your job is to make me look good."

What we want to say in reply (but never do) is: "Why should I work hard when you will take all the credit and look 'good'? I think I won't go the extra mile."

Or, "No, it's not. My job is to do *my* job. If you did your own job you wouldn't have to rely on others to look good, loser."

Studies show that the number-one factor in job satisfaction is the nature of the relationship with one's boss. The best managers don't take credit, they work with the team to share the credit.

So when the boss proclaims, "Your job is to make me look good," it's time to take stock of whether you want to deal with this boss. Life may be too short.

On Ditch Digging

When I escorted a bigwig C-level executive after a meeting, I was shocked at a comment he made. We were walking down the street to get into his town car to take him to his next meeting and passed a bunch of guys literally digging a ditch. They were decked out in hard hats and boots, having a great time, laughing and enjoying one another's company. The high-powered exec said, "I'd give anything to have a job like that."

Whoa. His suit probably cost more than all these guys make.

He spends all of his days in meetings. These guys could see the fruits of their labors and were proud of that fruit. They could start a job and finish a job.

Fruits of labor are a good thing. Too often, we spend our days draining e-mail or voice mail and wonder what we accomplished.

Think about that next time you get ready for work—what ditch can you dig?

Are We All Bosses?

The answer is yes. Okay, you may not be the CEO of Apple or AT&T, but you are the CEO of something. It could be your little work unit or your bowling league or your church group. At the very least, you are the CEO of your own life, your own career. You should act like you are that CEO and plan and act accordingly.

Some Authentic, Some, Not So Much

We laugh, but we are all guilty of using buzzwords. (Test: Have you used the phrase "At the end of the day" lately?) Most buzzwords get old and tired very fast, and though they may be mind numbingly repeated, some are worth integrating into our own usage:

- **It's complicated.** A perfect phrase to describe everything we now know about business and the universe. These two (or is it three?) simple words can answer any question: How is your love life? Worried about your job? Any luck with your project? How long do you think you will last in this job? The perfect answer that connotes substance but probably more than you need to know: It's complicated.

- **Fair enough.** Could be a comment, could be an answer, could be a question, and could be filler when no one else is saying anything. Could also mean you are a jerk and know nothing of what you say, but now you've said it so, "fair enough." It hits my list since it crops up often and can be used in so many ways.

- **Not so much.** A perfect description of life in the workplace that sins on the side of negativity without being offensive. Can easily be a proper response to questions like: Hey, do you like your new boss? Are you thinking about retiring on your 401(k) these days? Boy, those people in Washington are doing a good job, huh?

- **I'm good.** The most reassuring phrase out there that, too, has many meanings. When waiting to meet someone, if the receptionist asks if you want a coffee or water, the response can be, "I'm good." When falling off the roof while cleaning out the gutters and your wife asks if you are okay, the response can be the same, "I'm good." After a layoff, this is a desired response. A close relative to "I'm good" is "I got it." Can apply to catching a ball in center field or a way to say, "You don't have to say any more, I understand." It's a good phrase to employ to start doing and stop talking, which is always a good thing.

- **New normal.** Although way overused, this is a worthy phrase when it comes to reconciling expectations. For most of us, the new normal means the same way it used to be, just with a lot less.
- **That feels about right.** A welcome phrase used in any context, but especially welcome when asking for approval while in the front of a conference room giving a presentation. It implies "we could probably get more data but that won't make us any smarter so let's just go ahead, good work."

Then there are the phrases that will go away soon, and it will be too bad; they are good ones and some of my favorites:

- **Become a fan.** I like being a fan of the San Francisco Giants but I don't want to be a fan of Edna's scones or every restaurant where I ever had a cup of coffee.
- **Skill up.** I think this means get smarter and more equipped to do your job. Is that new?
- **Fat content.** I don't need any more reasons to feel guilty. When referring to an organization, there are better ways to describe too many people. Let me enjoy my cheesecake.
- **Narrow aperture.** I think this means focus on the most important things that need to be done. This is another phrase that makes me feel guilty for not paying attention in photography class.

Work today seems to be made up of ambiguous victories and nebulous defeats. Let's at least make life at work a little more bearable by using words and phrases that make us smile just a little.

People, Pay Attention

Which would you rather do? Have to sit through your annual performance review or get a root canal? In an informal poll, most people I asked voted for the root canal.

Few things induce more dread and anxiety than the performance review. It's easy to understand why: you know how you performed and you sit there and listen to your boss try to guess how you did. But I have a solution.

This year, keep track of what you do. Yes, if you don't want to feel like you're getting dental surgery, keep a simple list of your accomplishments, and when it's time for the review, whip the list out. Include everything. Yes, everything.

It doesn't have to be a fancy spreadsheet, but if you don't keep track, I guarantee you won't remember what you did a few months ago and you will be guessing about your performance just like your boss.

A review can be a time to take stock of your career and to consider whether or not you are working in the right place.

If your review is all about "Exceeds Expectations," it could be recognition for working your butt off or it may raise the question, is it too easy here?

A "Meets Expectations" designation means you are in the crowded pack. It means, too, that you should be asking yourself if you are working hard enough.

"Needs Improvement" means trouble, and that you really need to do a self-assessment. Don't try harder. Have a heart-to-heart with yourself to see if you need to change jobs or change careers.

Love the annual performance review because it is about *you*. it could change your life.

And who knows better than you what you did. You might even get a raise.

Death to Performance Reviews

HR professionals may be rolling their eyes with a sigh. Controlling managers may slam a fist on the desk. But cutting annual performance reviews out of the organizational psyche makes a ton of sense. It makes business sense; why do something year after year that everyone hates? Ask Accenture.

In an announcement that sent shivers through the world of "we've always done it this way," Accenture eliminated the annual performance review. The act was compared to eliminating a bout with the DMV each year or never again going for the annual teeth cleaning and check-up. On the "can this be true?" side, when the review process was eliminated it was like, ding-dong, the wicked witch is dead.

The annual review process is almost always viewed in the same way—as a necessary evil, a requirement that must be completed. For those receiving the review, it is viewed as a make-or-break annual assessment that may or may not be accurate and took an enormous amount of time. For those giving the reviews, it is seen as an annual series of torture-like meetings and sessions with results that may or may not be accurate and took an enormous amount of time. There was plenty of agreement about the onerous nature of the process and not as much agreement on the actual assessments that were given. So why continue to do it? Now we know that some big companies will not continue the process, and good for them.

The list of reasons that any company would make such a bold move is long.

First, there is a real business reason—do the math. Take a company that has fifty thousand employees. Assume that the time spent on each performance review is one hour (a low estimate) and that two people (the reviewee and the reviewer) are involved. Next, assume that, since time can be equated to a dollar amount of, let's say $100 per hour, the annual cost of reviews (at the very least) looks something like this formula:

50,000 employees × 2 people in each session = 100,000 hours × hourly rate of $100/hour = DO THE MATH.

Second, and more importantly, why continue a practice that no one likes, is seen as an annual ritual of pain, and may or may not be effective? Finally, someone asked the really hard question, "Why are we doing this?" And the answer was truthful. So the annual review is dead.

This is not to say that feedback is not a good thing. We should all look for some sort of feedback every day. The best source of feedback is our own inner self. People generally know how they perform and what should be improved. Feedback is still critically important.

We should ask others for feedback too, but that doesn't have to be in a formal review situation. The best feedback is usually in the hallway after a presentation or in the car on the way home from a sales call or after a meeting. Listen to that feedback and add your own inner analysis, and you will be a better performer.

The debate about feedback at work has been around for years. Do people really want feedback? Will they do anything with suggestions made in feedback sessions? What about negative feedback? Will that do anything more than hurt feelings?

We *all* want to hear positive feedback. It makes us feel great, whether we are or not. It can change a normal day into a special one. Most of us will say that feedback is welcome, as long as it is good. And then we chuckle about it.

But the truth is, the most helpful feedback is on the other side of the ledger. Feedback on areas that need improvement may not be welcome but sometimes it is what we need to hear, like it or not. The best boss I ever had gave me feedback every day and a lot of it was not good.

So, next time the areas for improvement come up, listen hard and don't be defensive. Feedback matters.

Frequent-Flier Miles and Other Addictions

"It's like heroin," is a phrase that is now part of the organizational lexicon. The reference is not about drugs, although that is possible. The phrase refers to any number of work and tech activities that have become addictions. Anything with a screen is now an addiction, but addictions are more pervasive than just the screens. Other current addictions include conference calls, meetings, 1000-calorie coffee drinks every day at 9:00 a.m., taking work home, texting, and e-mails.

It is possible to have fun without sharing the fun on social media. It is possible to have a romantic dinner without glancing at the phone every two minutes. It is possible to spend an evening with the family talking. In fact, the possibilities are limitless if you can pull yourself away from the addictions that can rule our life and make it less rich.

Pings, Pangs, Buzzes, and Vibrations— Productivity Reminders

I have lived the ritual. I have seen the ritual a thousand times. The day goes like this…you get to the work space and turn on the computer; it pings to attention. You sit down, enter your password, and it pangs with approval. You go to the kitchen, grab your coffee out of the Keurig K-Cup coffeemaker when it buzzes, and then sit down. But before you get into the details of the spreadsheets, your phone vibrates with a text from your mom that you need to read. Also, you need to check Facebook. Wow, there is a new "10 Celebrity Facts You Need to Know." Ugh, too hard to navigate. Back to FB, never mind, always the same people. Let's see what's going on with my Twitter feed. Then, a glance at People.com to see what's new with the royal family, and finally, on to e-mails. You look up and it's after 10 a.m. Time for another coffee.

It is impossible to go through a day without dealing with hundreds of distractions that kill productivity.

Connectivity is the problem. We seek connectivity, and we are frustrated when it is not available, but it can be a productivity wasteland. When one is connected, the constant pinging of e-mails and notifications and texts is like mosquitos buzzing around the bedroom—you have to deal with them. Those enticing tidbits we receive every day are just too damn interesting to ignore. The constant "urgent updates" about NBA coaches getting into fisticuffs or "Why Elephants Rarely Get Cancer" are just as addictive as crack cocaine. And opening one of those tidbits is like pulling on a string of a sweater—it may never end. The fighting NBA coaches will lead to athletes in jail, which will lead to your alma mater website, which will lead to your old friends, which will lead you to a cat playing the piano, and so on and so forth.

Stop. All the requests and pings from LinkedIn, Facebook, Instagram, Twitter, and other addictions that require *immediate* attention can wait. The Nigerian prince who needs a bank account number is always with us. It never ends.

The best productivity hack is to disconnect. I know it is impossible, but for an hour during the day, disconnect to get real work done.

I have a writer friend who gets up each day and locks himself in a dark closet with no Internet connection. He takes his laptop in there with him but does not ever connect. His job is to write. He stays in the closet until he has written one thousand words.

Think about how productive some airplane trips have been for you. Web access is spotty, if available at all, so we can put on noise-cancelling earphones and work on the project, the book, the plan, the spreadsheet, or one of the important activities that is usually interrupted but requires focus and concentration. Although counterintuitive, airplane time can be productive because of the disconnection.

There are no tricks to being disconnected other than disconnecting. No matter the job, at the end of the year we are measured in production. You need to know how production is defined. Is it in dollars? Clients? Saves? Points? Customer service? Widgets made? Hours? The list of productivity measures is almost infinite. I doubt that knowing about Kim Kardashian is one of those measures. Disconnect to be more productive.

I don't know of anyone who has made a major scientific discovery between the constant pinging of e-mails. I don't know of anyone who has written a great book while the Twitter feed is clinking along. I don't know of anyone who is not distracted by the buzz of a text. For me, I know that productivity is connected to being disconnected.

Business Travel Tango

I've had coffee spilled on my head. I've had computers drop out of overhead compartments onto my head. I've had a seat jammed backward so hard that it broke my computer. I've been in the middle seat between two large brothers who talked to each other the entire flight.

Now the issue of whether or not airline seats should recline is front and center. The question of whether or not to recline has resulted in fistfights, emergency landings, and security issues. We all agree that life on the road is not glamorous. As a road warrior I am often asked for advice on business travel, so here are a few simple tips:

- Never travel with your boss on a flight that lasts more than one hour.
- Although offers are tantalizing, upgrades never really happen.
- Always go into a Zen mode when travelling.
- And last—don't go. There is often no real need. Do the conference call instead.

The Big Work Lie: "Out of Office"...REALLY?

It happens to all of us. You send an e-mail that requires a reply. You might even add some sizzle to it with a big red exclamation point. Could be a request to fix a problem. Could be something really urgent, and you are desperate for an answer. Could be an appointment or a meeting request.

Within a second of hitting the "send" button, you hear the ping of a new e-mail and see the response: "Automatic Reply—Out of Office," followed by, "I will be out of the office until _____ and will have limited e-mail access. If this is an emergency, please contact _____."

That response raises lots of eyebrows and generates lots of questions, mainly, "Do we believe that response? Is he or she *really* out of touch? With today's devices, is it even possible to be *really* out of the office and out of touch? Does that mean the recipient is *really* not checking? Is it true that people are truly addicted to e-mail? So let's wait and see...

Sure enough, within just a few minutes, the person who posted the out-of-office note is sending a response. And it's a good, thoughtful response that addresses the issue. The response is not, "Buzz off! I am in Hawaii with my family and I haven't had a vacation in five years." The thoughtful response raises a new question: Why did the person bother to create the out-of-office status if he took the office with him?

No one believes the out-of-office status anymore. No matter where we are, what we are doing, and whom we are with, we all sneak time to check and respond to e-mail. Worse, we all expect others to do the same. No place is safe and no one believes that you are not checking e-mails, even while on vacation. It could be the tragedy of today's workplace but it is the reality, and it is not a good thing.

We should reconsider the out-of-office designation and use it as it was intended. That is, we are out! Maybe just adding the word "really" would help. As in, "I am REALLY out of the office and REALLY will not be checking e-mail and would REALLY appreciate it if you didn't bug me and REALLY want you to deal with my colleague _____, whom I REALLY do trust to handle things while I am gone. REALLY." I bet that would really do it.

Out of office should make a comeback, but it only works if we take the status to heart and personally enforce it. We all need a break, and studies are showing that disconnecting makes us more productive when we do reconnect. We need to take time out of the office to get away from it all. We need to preserve out of office, but only in its truest sense.

Some love the out-of-office status, but they have abused it. They use it too much so it makes it hard to believe and not relevant. I know people who post the out-of-office status when it really means "Out to lunch, be back in an hour." Those people should discover Twitter.

Others want to preserve the status because they use it as an ego thing, as in, "I am out of the office on a Polynesian island with my supermodel girlfriend through the end of the summer. If there is blood involved, call my people and I may get back to you."

Remember those pink slips with the header "While You Were Out"? There used to be stacks of those on desks with names and phone numbers scribbled on them. They are long gone. I fear the out-of-office status is not far behind, so let's bring it back in its truest meaning.

In the meantime, my advice is when you need to take a break, post the out-of-office status but add the word REALLY. Maybe it will work, and your health, both mental and physical, will thank you. Or, only take vacations in places where there is no Internet access. If you can find one.

The E-Mail Thing

I overheard a guy in the elevator talking about how many e-mails he was receiving every day. At first, I suffered from e-mail envy. Whoa, this guy must be important. I wondered if he counted e-mails from Nigerian princes and Expedia.

Then it occurred to me, those hundreds of e-mails he was bragging about were not a good thing. He can win that contest. It's like someone boasting about having millions of frequent-flier miles.

There is a simple rule when it comes to e-mail. The more you send, the more you receive. If you don't want to receive so many, don't send so many. I am not suggesting you go off the grid, I am saying that if you are one of the crazy people who sends hundreds, of course you will get hundreds of responses. Call it Moran's Law of e-mail reciprocity.

Of course there are plenty of e-mails that need to be sent and ones that require responses. "Unresponsive" is never a word you want on a performance review.

E-mail is the greatest invention since yellow stickies but it is not a measure of performance.

So to all of who keep e-mail scores or have e-mail envy. Get over it.

Those Best Companies

Fortune magazine just released its new report of the "100 Best Companies to Work For." To me, this is the annual report of work envy. You guessed it, I don't work for any of these companies.

The magazine shows photos of very happy people who are usually thin, diverse, and good looking. These same people use their spare time to save the world through volunteering. Some of these companies allow people to bring their dogs to work and even the dogs look happy.

The companies on the list offer day care, cappuccinos, car cleaning, free healthy snacks, cool-looking furniture, and health clubs with spas. That sounds like a vacation to me.

I bet the companies on the list get lots of applications and can pick the cream of the crop.

But every day I hear reports of how many people are out of work and looking for a job. Many have given up on even looking for a job and are desperate. Next year, I would like to see *Fortune* publish the list of the "100 Companies That Are Hiring and Will Offer a Fair Wage and Especially Want Good People Who Are Desperate."

Hello, My Name Is . . .

Any big hotel town is loaded with conventioneers. We love to have them in town, and it's tough not to recognize them. No, they are not wearing crazy hats and Mardi Gras beads; they are wearing big old fancy nametags. Gone are the days when the tag was a sticker with a big "HELLO, MY NAME IS..." on it. The nametag today is wrapped in plastic and hangs around the neck like a badge of honor. Some have a bunch of ribbons hanging down like war medals. The ribbons proclaim SPEAKER or SPONSOR or VENDOR. VIP is not enough.

It's one thing when security makes you wear that big VISITOR tag that makes you feel like a tourist. You are stuck, and it is your admission ticket. The rest of the time, take the nametags off when you are not roaming around those Grand Ballrooms. You will have more fun.

About Those Weekends

A fan writes in with a question: "Almost every Saturday morning I receive an e-mail from my boss. The e-mail starts out with this greeting: I hope you *had* a good weekend. Then he proceeds to ask me to do a bunch of tasks in advance of Monday. What do you think I should do? Signed, Weekend Worrier."

Dear Worrier: this is a complicated question.

The simplest solution is to not check your e-mails on weekends. I doubt you will do that if you want to keep your job.

Or you could tell your boss to stop sending Saturday morning e-mails. That could lead to a bad ending too.

Or you could resolve to change jobs, but there are probably e-mails there too.

Everyone is now checking in all the time. How you handle all the requests and distractions will dictate how much you like your job.

Almost always, most things can wait.

Red Licorice Can Kill Your Organization

While sitting in a company lobby recently, I watched a young man who works at the place duck into the break room, reach into the Red Vines tub, and stuff a big batch of them into his backpack. Then he stuffed a printer cartridge into the backpack. This is called stealing.

Anonymous surveys show that between 40 and 75 percent of workers steal everything from Post-it Notes to toilet paper. (Really, people, toilet paper?!)

It's not a good thing in so many ways. There is the stealing thing, but the biggest problem is the culture that is created. Stealing a few pencils may not seem like much but it sets the standard and tone of the organization. It's not okay. Corporate cultures are formed by what is accepted as well as what is prescribed. Plus, who wants to work with thieves?

Keep the sticky fingers off the sticky notes.

The Backpack Is the New Briefcase

The definition of business casual has changed. So has the definition of the thing we use to transport our work stuff around. That thing is the backpack. When the little kids line up for the school bus I can see Dora the Explorer—and SpongeBob SquarePants—embellished backpacks. When the older kids hang out on the quad I can spot the backpacks from JanSport and The North Face. When I'm lining up for the flight from San Francisco to JFK, the line is loaded with men and women, dressed like they just left the boardroom, slinging backpacks over their shoulders. Hmmmm.

Backpacks are now a major accessory for the businessperson. I suspect it all started when people right out of college refused to change. The transition from college to the real world is tough enough without having to abandon one's favorite backpack. In fact, some big firms began to dispense backpacks to new employees with the company logo branded on one of the pockets. The geeks refused to give up their beloved backpacks, and as they grew older and got into management, the backpacks came with them.

Backpacks are everywhere and, wow, have they changed. The Tickle Me Elmo backpack is out. The choice of backpack style is infinite. I just received a catalogue that features a $1,200 backpack for busy executives. The merits of such an expensive backpack may be lost on me.

Some that I see wear a backpack to work as if they are in survival training. Those backpacks are loaded with water bottles and carabineers hanging from them. You never know when you might need climbing equipment at work. Best to leave the grappling hooks for the weekend backpack.

Other backpacks tromping onto the elevator behind someone look like those that are on their way to do battle in a major conflict. Each little pocket and nook and cranny is packed with unknown goodies required for survival on the battlefield. This level of sophistication is usually not needed.

Some backpacks look like they weigh a ton, some look empty. Backpacks can smack you in the elevator or while waiting in line at the coffee shop. On airplanes, the backpack in the aisle is a lethal weapon as they swing around behind unknowing travelers. Be careful not to hurt people with the backpack.

But the questions about backpacks remain:

1. Is there an age limit to wearing a backpack? Probably not, but the backpack you choose should be age appropriate. As a leader, anything you wear or say sends out a signal to those around you. A backpack is not different. As you get older, others might assume you are wearing one to save the wear and tear on your back. And that assumption is probably correct.

2. Is there an image limit to wearing a backpack? Would the CEO of General Electric wear a backpack? I doubt it. Would the CEO of Facebook wear a backpack? Maybe. I don't know the answer but the image question lingers. Does a senior exec schlep around so much stuff that he or she needs a backpack? Probably not.

Alternatives to backpacks are still available. The alternatives like messenger bags and computer bags are equally important to your persona.

You probably need a backpack. A backpack makes it easier to carry all the necessities of life in transit and at work: the laptop, a water bottle, and snacks. A laptop is travel friendly. It fits under the seat in front of you or on the back of the scooter. A backpack lets you use both hands to use your phone. A backpack says as much about you as your shoes or your hairstyle, and can help your image.

I am all for anything that makes life at work easier, saves your back, and enhances your style. But like everything else at work, your backpack will say something about you. Be alert.

Unequal Distance

Just about anyone who does any travelling for business will eventually be in New York City. It's the big time, and for the business traveler it's a sign that you are in the major leagues. But the perception by those in the East about the West is slightly skewed.

On a call with a New Yorker the other day, the person asked, "What time is it out there?"

Out there? She asked it like I was on Mars. Then it occurred to me. To a lot of people on the East Coast, we on the West Coast are like a distant planet. We are very interesting but way too far to visit. Why do New Yorkers think it is easier and closer for us to travel to New York than it is for them to travel west? Like airline ticket pricing, it is one of the mysteries of modern business travel.

Ever hear a suggestion from a New Yorker that we "meet in the middle"? And then they suggest Pittsburgh? Or the geographically enlightened think Chicago. Chicago is not in the middle.

As a San Franciscan, I think Denver is more in the middle.

Travel Disasters I Have Known

The contest I don't want to enter is for who has the most business travel disaster stories. I might win. Anyone who has spent time in consulting, sales, or another "travel required" field is in the same boat. No one wants to tell the worst story.

But while we are on the subject, there is one particular trip that I remember well. I had to be in Manhattan for an important Monday-morning meeting so was on a red-eye flight on a Sunday from San Francisco to New York—start there, in the disaster category. Something went afoul in the reservation process and I was re-ticketed to a middle seat in the last row of coach, right next to the bathrooms. I was seated next to a person who was traveling with a cat in a small bag. I am allergic to cats. There was a medical emergency so we landed in Chicago to drop off a passenger, meaning we were delayed into New York. Being late, I had to take a "sink shower" at JFK and change into my suit and tie surrounded by others in the lavatory. I took a stressful taxi ride into the city and arrived just in time to be notified that my client had cancelled the meeting.

There were many trips like that, and after a while one becomes inured to the indignities. But along the way you learn many tricks from fellow road warriors. Experienced business travelers usually don't want to share secrets of travel, especially with the newbies. I see newbies searching for electrical outlets and overhear them talking about Marriott Rewards points. It is refreshing to see people excited about business travel. It doesn't last long.

Any frequent traveler knows the one with the most frequent-flier miles is not the winner. Those of us who are always on airplanes are conditioned to have low expectations and to deal with whatever comes our way. We develop a certain set of instincts that protects us from disappointment and prepares us for the war that is business travel. We can look at a gate agent and know without asking that the flight is delayed or that hoping for an upgrade is useless.

Every frequent traveler develops a unique dance to deal with the vagaries and challenges the road presents. To help with the dance, here are a few suggestions from the unwritten Guide to Business Travel:

- At security, **always get behind the guy in line wearing loafers.** Or, put another way, get in the line with other road warriors. Avoid the spot behind the family with the strollers.
- **Never check a bag, ever.** If you have too much stuff for a carry-on, dump it out and start all over. It's not about the fees or the schlep factor, it's about the flexibility in changing flights. If you want to change flights, which you will, the first question the gate agent will ask is, "Did you check a bag?"
- **The seat pocket in front of you is not your friend.** Anything you place in the handy pocket, like eyeglasses, passports, tickets, or presentations, will eventually be lost and never retrieved. Airlines are not known for effective lost and found departments.
- **Set expectations on upgrades.** Being on a list is not the same as having a seat. Flying on Monday mornings or Thursday evenings means you are lucky to have a seat at all.
- **Bring reading material.** No matter how much work there is to do, breaks are essential and you never know how long the flight will really take. Bring a book to read, either a paper one or one loaded on a device. *People* magazine doesn't count.
- **Wear earphones.** Nothing says, "I don't want to talk to you" like a big set of earphones. Plus, the airline earphones are not very good.
- **Be alert for bad news.** Certain travel words should set your hairs on end in anticipation that things are about to go downward. So finally, for those less traveled, I submit the most dreaded words for the business traveler. These utterances usually come from the cockpit but, given technology, can now come in a text or from another weary traveler.
  - Unfortunately
  - Good news, bad news (it's never really good)
  - Shuttle bus
  - Talking to maintenance
  - Reservation was not guaranteed
  - System problems
  - Storm
  - The president is in town
  - We've been notified by ATC

And the most dreaded of all:

- That bag needs to be checked

After hearing the words, we sigh resignedly and do what we are told. Sometimes going into the Zen mode is all there is to do.

Travel shouldn't be the hard part of the job but sometimes it is. All we want is to get to where we need to be, or, most importantly, get home. In between, the work gets done.

Business Travel Things

An etiquette question: When you are on an airplane trying to work and the person in front of you slams the chair back into your space so that you can no longer use your laptop, what is the proper etiquette to show one's displeasure?

Should one:

Kick the chair as hard as you can so it goes back into the proper upright position and gives you two more inches of space?

Write a letter to the airline complaining of the rudeness of the person sitting in front of you?

Pour hot coffee over the head of that reclining person? Or,

Slam your own seat back so that the person sitting behind you is subjected to the same affront that you are?

These options are all real and have all been done. What is so bothersome is that, through careful engineering, if the person in front of you does recline the seat, it is impossible to use a laptop. Those two inches could make the difference in career success.

The solution is to stay off airplanes. You will be a lot more productive.

Ambiguous Victories and Nebulous Defeats

Rare is the day when we complete a difficult project. It is not often that we say we had a truly great day at work. Most days are not great and not terrible. High highs and low lows are probably rare. Most days are in the middle. That is, just another day. But days are not "just" days. Time is finite, and we should try to derive at least a little satisfaction each day. The best way to do that is to convert nebulous defeats into ambiguous victories. A nebulous defeat is all the glancing blows that fill our day and can ruin it. Things like an e-mail with a tone that is slightly offensive or a meeting that was a big waste of time. If you let all the nebulous defeats pile up and get to you, life will be miserable.

Instead, find the ambiguous victories, like a customer who loved how you handled a transaction or catching up on e-mail before the end of the day. The slight change in your way of thinking may mean the difference in how you think about work and yourself.

Let's Improve Morale Around Here

We hear it all the time—employee morale is important! Every time I turn around, there is a new study or research report that tells me so. Happy people make for an effective workplace. But how can you tell if people are happy or unhappy at work?

I guess you can tell if morale is good—people are singing in their cubes and dancing at the cappuccino machine.

Low morale isn't hard to detect either. Of course, there is absenteeism. People don't show up when morale is low. Another indicator is a very high volume of Dilbert cartoons. But my favorite sign is in the parking lot: when all the cars are backed in to parking spots for a fast exit, it's a sure sign that morale could improve.

Truth is, morale is really hard to pin down and it changes all the time.

Like U.S. Supreme Court Justice Potter Stewart said about pornography, I can't define morale but I know it when I see it, good or bad. Rejoice when it is positive and ask why when morale is terrible.

Is Sitting the New Smoking?

The standing desk craze is sweeping the world and can now be seen at organizations large and small. A standing desk is just a really tall desk with no chair, and models come in all shapes and sizes. The research is pointing to all sorts of benefits we can derive from not sitting down all day.

Working while standing up will burn eighty to one hundred calories an hour, improves blood flow, alleviates back pain, strengthens muscles, and actually boosts productivity. Wow. So I tried it.

I learned that sore feet and sore legs can go along with all that standing. Plus, I felt like I was lurking over all my colleagues, who were comfortably seated. I saw them glancing at me like I was in air traffic control.

What I've learned is that activity matters. During the day, get off your duff and get the blood flowing. If you don't get up you may be stricken with Silicon Valley Syndrome. Yes, it has an official name and if you have it you are achy, your back hurts, you have trouble sleeping, and your head is pounding. Silicon Valley Syndrome is the physical and mental health symptoms that arise from spending WAY too much time sitting in front of a computer screen. Operative word is sitting.

It has taken me years to figure out how my chair works and now I know that spending time in it is bad for me. Sounds like the cure is stand-up desks, or maybe just not going to work at all. Your body will thank you.

When Is Starting Early Starting *Too* Early?

When my daughter was six months old I took her to the local health club to sign her up for swimming lessons.

The nice clerk signing her up asked me, "Is she a beginner?" Remember, she was six months old. I was riddled with guilt that she was already behind the curve and I had let her down. She turned out to be a great swimmer, even though, according to some, I guess she started late.

Which brings me to an invitation I just received to talk to a bunch of sixth graders about careers. It seems a little early to me. When I was in sixth grade, careers were not high on the list of things I wanted to chat about. Video games, yes. Baseball yes. Academic requirements of becoming a dentist, no.

But, like swimming, I know there is a push today to start thinking about careers early.

So, for all you sixth graders and others seeking early, or maybe late, career advice, here it is: do your math homework.

Stop Reminding Me

Through the beauty of technology, each day I wake up to a slew of reminders. I bet you do too.

I am reminded that my password is expiring on a website I didn't know existed. I am reminded that the birthdays of ten people are approaching. Except I don't think I ever met any of the ten people. I am reminded that Father's Day or Groundhog Day is coming and that I should buy something to commemorate the holiday.

The worst ones are when I am reminded that I cannot fly to Fiji tomorrow, even though someone is offering me a good rate. And then there are the notes that broadcast that so-and-so hit the IPO jackpot and I am reminded that I didn't hit that jackpot.

At work, the best reminders come from my colleagues and clients. We all want to be reminded that we are doing something worthwhile and valued and that our contributions make a difference.

Remember that next time you delete all those other reminders.

Please Stop Doing Stupid Shit

It is not for me to judge others, but I do see things in and around the workplace that make me scratch my head. What I see has encouraged me to start a new national campaign. It is the STOP DOING STUPID SHIT campaign. There are generals who send flirtatious e-mails. There are heads of spy agencies who spend too much time with biographers. There are CEOs who break company policy with coworkers. There are holy men who drive drunk. There are just too many examples right now.

Every time a leader resigns for inappropriate behavior or questionable judgment, it sends shivers through the ranks of other leaders.

Questions are pondered: Did the photo that I tweeted of my bare ass go through to the right person? Was that forged receipt on the expense account for too much? How drunk was I at the holiday party? Why don't I remember what happened at the trade show? Will anyone notice that I used the company computer to check out the latest porn site?

Break a rule, a policy, or the law, or just plain use bad judgment—you will get caught. The list of those who seem to have forgotten that simple truth is long and it grows every day. It seems that men have a much more difficult time understanding this rule than women.

We *all* do stupid stuff sometimes. We use the office computer inappropriately. We send or read e-mails that are off color. We do things we wish we hadn't. But, just like all the generals and the CEOs and all the others, you will get caught.

To join the Stop Doing Stupid Shit Campaign, just stop doing stupid shit.

Lunchtime Stress

I am all for getting out of the office and enjoying a midday break. Having a sandwich or salad with colleagues can be both refreshing and build the team. Or that's the way it used to be.

Lots of restaurants today can make having lunch as stressful as giving a presentation. The food might be good but the act of ordering it can be like a lie detector test. While standing in line you try to choose among hundreds of permutations and options. But before you are ready someone is shouting at you, NEXT, NEXT! Those in line behind you cough nervously or shuffle their feet. THEY must know what they want.

Once you've ordered, you may get a flashing device to tell you when your food is ready.

Then, when you have the food in hand, there is nowhere to sit.

We still love you, lunch, stress and all.

Is Cycling the New Golf?

Cycling is now the place where business is done outside of the office, at least for the young business crowd. Cyclists are everywhere, whizzing by in big packs, shouting over their shoulders about the latest deal. I see them everywhere. I don't see golfers unless I am golfing.

I don't see golf clubs in the corner of any company lobby but I see lots of bikes.

A bicycle can be transportation, your exercise, and your show of style. Bike outfits are trendy and tight. Golf outfits are not that different from business casual. It is difficult to be embarrassed on a bike. The golf course is a different story.

Regarding the time commitment, a bike ride can be ten minutes. Golf can take all day. Maybe I need to go bike shopping.

Oh, Those Sick Days

Ever wonder why people show up at work even when they are sick as a dog? I just heard a report that claims that upward of 70 percent of employees still go to work when they know they are sick.

I'm not surprised—there are very good reasons for this phenomenon.

The first is the very legitimate fear that if you are not at work everyone will say, "Hey, we did fine without him, do we really need him?" If you are worried about your job, there's nothing like being absent to increase that fear.

Another reason that people show up, in spite of sneezing every thirty seconds, is to get out of the house and away from the kids. Who do you want to give your germs to, the jerk in the cube next to you or your kids?

And for some, there is always the "I need the money" reason to show up.

I recommend that if you are sick, it's time to catch up with the latest on CNN.

How About Gender Appearance Equity?

Let's see... Mark Zuckerberg of Facebook wears jeans and a hoodie every day. It's his trademark. Steve Jobs wore blue jeans and a black mock turtleneck every day. It was the ultimate cool. A venture capitalist I know wears black every day. When I asked him if he was making a statement, he replied, "No, I'm too lazy to figure out what to wear every day." Most guys wear some variation of khakis and a checkered shirt every day and do just fine.

Hmmmm. What about women at work? Wearing the same thing every day is not cool or a trademark. It's probably seen as some sort of career liability. When it comes to work apparel, guys just have it easier.

I don't keep track of such things but in so many career areas women just have a higher degree of difficulty to succeed. The wardrobe shouldn't be one of those.

Guilty As Charged

One of my many goals in life is to eliminate guilt. But technology seems to be taking my goal in the wrong direction.

I feel guilty for not being up to date on all the new gadgets. Was I supposed to get that 4G, or is it a 5G phone now? My old one still works, though.

The biggest guilt inducer is e-mail. Even with a very strong spam filter on, every day I peek at tons of e-mails that make me feel guilty.

There is 50 percent off on domain names and I probably need a few of those.

Teamwork 101 and CRM webinars are going on later today! I need to know about these things.

There are ten ways to retire now and I was just thinking about retiring.

And there are all those five-star hotels that are missing my visits. They might go out of business if I don't travel!

Embedded between all of these guilt inducers is real work that makes me feel guilty too.

Maybe I should just stop checking e-mail so much.

But that would make me feel guilty.

That Permanent Record

We all have our viewpoints about politics, real estate, waterboarding, Donald Trump, and the definition of pornography. Some of us might be right, but how do we share our viewpoints?

I can tell you one platform not to use for sharing: your work e-mail. E-mails from real companies hit my screen every day from real executives in which they are bashing someone or something, and often not very politely. Then there is that genre of off-color jokes and worse that are tough to spot when they come from a work address—after the e-mail is open, it's too late.

Urban legend has it that someone is monitoring all those e-mails broadcast from your work address. Hard to imagine a more boring job but the truth is, and I shouldn't have to tell people this, the record of those e-mails is in a server somewhere and it can be monitored.

That high school teacher was right. There is a "permanent record," and your e-mails are in it. Share all you want, just don't do it from your work e-mail account.

Remember the time your second-grade teacher caught you throwing a spitball and threatened, "This will show up on your permanent record!" I imagined a file in the principal's office where my very own permanent record lived for the time being. I thought it would follow me forever, so I needed to keep it perfect. I saw it as a thick brown folder labeled Permanent Record. The logistics of how it would follow me for a lifetime were a little fuzzy but I lived in trepidation of bad things showing up and haunting me for life. I was pleased to learn the principal didn't hold any permanent record.

But wait, it's back! My permanent record has reemerged. My second-grade teacher was right! Does it matter what shows up in that record? The answer is yes.

If you don't believe me, ask any senior leader who is being vetted for a job. There is a permanent record. It is called the Internet.

Calling All Characters

When I talk about characters, I am not talking about weirdos who disrupt things. I am talking about people with a sense of humor and a different perspective; people who have crazy ideas that just might help; people who ask the questions that no one else will ask and people who don't wear khaki pants and checkered blue shirts every day.

Characters can help your organization and make it much more interesting. Some call it diversity.

The Boss Is Back

Why do we like our jobs? What is it that creates job satisfaction? These are cosmic questions that researchers have been poring over since the dawn of work. And there are a lot of answers.

Sure, pay and benefits are up there. The nature of the work is very important, since it is the line of work you've chosen. But one factor seems to always stand out, and it may surprise you. It's your boss. Yes, that boss.

The more you feel supported by your boss, and the more you feel mentored by your boss, and the more you get along with your boss, the more satisfied you will be at work.

Of course, if the converse is true you will probably hate your job—and your boss.

But I think bosses are almost always trying to do the right thing. You might just need to remind your boss of how important he or she is to your job satisfaction.

Are You Happy?

Lists dominate the news feed on the Internet. The lists range from "The Top One Hundred Colleges" to "Three Ways to Tell If Your Spouse Is Cheating." Then there are the lists about the happiest people at work, the most satisfied workers, and the best careers in the world. To me, these are the lists intended to make us feel unhappy and dissatisfied.

Almost all studies point to clergy being number one on the happiness scale. I guess the least worldly are the happiest of all. Number two is almost always firefighters. They have the best of both worlds: they are both heroes and helpers. Rounding out the top group are physical therapists, authors, and special ed teachers.

These studies also point out those who hate their jobs, just in case we need to feel worse that we are not in the clergy. These lists almost always include titles like director of IT, director of sales and marketing, product manager, senior web developer, technical specialist, and law clerk. Funny that the pay is much better and these jobs have higher social status than the most satisfying ones.[2]

I don't need research reports to tell me the obvious: people who hate their jobs feel imprisoned in bureaucracies. They don't derive a sense of worth from their efforts. The organizations they work for don't know where they add value and as a result, neither do these people.

Whoa. Get those career change thoughts revved up.

Reason to Be Thankful at Work

When we give thanks, it is usually for the love of our family and friends and for the joy of the largesse we can share. In so many ways, Thanksgiving is a time for real reflection and appreciation. And that should be enough, but then there is that work thing.

So each year during the Thanksgiving holiday, I try to find a few tidbits about work for which we can be thankful. When it comes to workplace thanks, it is easier for some to be thankful than others. But, as always, we all have some things to be thankful for when it comes to the workplace.

■ We can be thankful for the Internet and the knowledge of the universe it can provide when it comes to work research. We can also be thankful for the piano-playing cats.

■ We can be thankful for all the technologies like conference calls and Skype that allow us to stay off airplanes for business travel. And be thankful for good earphones that block out the crazy guy in the cube next door and let us listen to our favorite music.

■ We can be thankful that business casual is now more the norm than the exception.

■ If we have a good boss who supports us and mentors us, we should be very thankful. Having a good boss is always the number-one factor in job satisfaction.

■ If we enjoy our colleagues at work and learn from them and can't wait to be around them, we should be really thankful. If not, find a new group and be thankful that there are alternatives.

■ If we derive a real sense of worth and purpose from our work, and we get paid for it too, that's as good as it gets. Be thankful.

- If we have a job with health-care benefits, where free coffee with real cream is provided, and the possibility of a promotion exists, be thankful.

- And most of all, be thankful if your organization has an IT guy who can fix whatever damage we do on a daily basis.

So put the smartphone down, even for a minute, and enjoy it.

Fist Bumping

Much is being made of the fist bump today. You know, the fist bump is when you make a fist and bump the fist of the person you are greeting. Presidents are doing it. Oprah recommends it. And the researchers are jumping on the bandwagon.

Through a series of tests, researchers in Wales documented that fist bumps are twenty times more hygienic than handshakes. They are also ten times cleaner than high fives.

Has the fist bump spread into the workplace yet? Not so much. Imagine meeting the new CEO and greeting him or her with a fist bump.

Too bad. It might not only save some sick days but could avoid the handshake contest of who's got the stronger grip. With fist bumps, neither bumper has the upper hand, so to speak.

Researchers say the fist bump is spreading because it signals triumph and approval. And at work, we need more of that.

The Importance of Being Urgent

A harried manager told me the other day that he was having trouble separating the critical, the urgent, the top priorities, and worst of all, what he described as the DO this ASAP!

He said his e-mail was so full of red exclamation points that he thought his hair might catch on fire. This is a guy not having any fun at work.

Is it a way of life in the complex workplace these days? I don't think so.

Some say the secret of life is enjoying the passage of time. I say the secret at work is being able to discern the truly urgent from the "it can wait and maybe it will go away" category.

The daily choice of piling stress on and working like a madman or setting priorities is the secret to success today.

A simple question to ask is, should I move a hundred things an inch this month or just a few things a mile this month?

The answer might help you separate what's burning from what's just on slow simmer.

What Matters?

A student in a management class recently asked me a very simple question: What matters? Meaning, at work, what is important?

A crazy class discussion ensued. The answers to the simple question ranged all over the map. Some said connections matter. Some said knowing technology. Some said being analytical and knowing how to read spreadsheets. Some said looking good and going to the right school. A lone voice said knowing how to write and communicate matters. In fact, everyone had an answer and they were all correct because what matters is different for each of us based on where we know we can contribute. And we can all contribute.

What matters is your ability to assess what is important and make a contribution in that direction. What matters is a simple question with a simple answer: what matters is what you can do to make the organization better. That's what you need to know.

Last Call

The relationships we form at work are important. It's the relationships that make us like our job—or not. And lots of times our best friends are the people we meet at work. It's a good and natural thing.

When we show up we look for friends to chat about the new boss or the home team or the latest headline. A good work friend is the person who is a teacher and is so reliable that we count on him or her for cover.

It would be good to make more friends at work. But when all we do is look at a computer screen all day and eat turkey sandwiches at our desk, it's hard to do.

Every once in a while, someone will come along who makes the place better. And when that person retires, we are all a little bit less. We should all try to be that person.

Special
Holiday Bonus Section

Holidays at Work

Holidays at work can create a set of issues that are just as confusing as business casual. For example, when a holiday lands on a weekend, or is always on the third Thursday of November, there is never a decision to make. But when a holiday moves around every year like a wounded bird, the decisions surrounding that holiday can create planning havoc. When a holiday lands on a Wednesday the mind starts to spin. What's a loyal employee to do?

If I only take that Wednesday off, that's not much of a holiday. But I bet a lot people will take off Thursday and Friday too. That would make for a quiet office and maybe I can get real work done.

Or, maybe I should take off Monday and Tuesday before the holiday. But then the holiday will feel like a Sunday because I have to go back to work on Thursday.

Another alternative is taking the day before and after the holiday off. No, that would be weird to work on just the Monday and Friday of the week. Who ever heard of that?

Wait, I have an idea: I'll just take off the entire week. I am sure I will have a lot of company. Got it? To help with holiday thinking and the nuances surrounding each one, it's best to create clarity around the holiday thing. Doing right around the holidays might be just as important to getting promoted as doing right around performance review time.

Holiday Party Dos and Don'ts

Wow, the years go by and everything changes except the potential for bad behavior at the company holiday party. So it's that time of year to remind everyone about holiday party protocol. The rules are simple:

> Dance with your boss's spouse at your peril. There is lot to lose and not much to gain.
>
> Remember that anything crazy you do will end up on YouTube. It will become part of your permanent record, so to speak.
>
> Dress as if you are going to a very festive wedding, not like you are going to a Halloween party.
>
> Take a taxi or Uber if you have too much to drink. Arrest records are a lot less funny on Monday morning.
>
> Thank everyone you meet and say that you are happy to be a part of the team, even if it's not true.

Then there is the "new" holiday party, or, as some call it, lunch. For reasons of cost and, more importantly, liability, many holiday parties are now lunch. Yes, look around at lunch during the holiday season and you might see a large group sitting around the long table. At the head of the table the boss is awkwardly making small talk. Everyone else is sitting awkwardly too. A few gifts might be exchanged.

If the company is really generous, everyone will be given the rest of the afternoon off.

More likely, after the holiday party, it's back to the grind.

The new holiday party may be boring. But at least you don't have to worry about drinking too much and that sinking feeling when you don't remember what you said to the boss at the party.

Have a happy holiday party and order the most expensive thing on the menu. Whether it's a drunken bacchanal or lunch, the last rule for holiday parties is to go and have a good time. You will be missed.

A Holiday Missive

Like everyone else who owns a computer, I receive a lot of electronic holiday greetings. All are well-meaning and sincere. Some of the senders I even know. Although this message, too, is from a stranger and is a broadcast message, I hope you will glean from it some true holiday spirit.

You worked hard all year, so take a break if you can; you deserve it. Like all recent times, the new year will be crazy and full of opportunities for growth and exciting work. Look forward to it.

Although those e-mail holiday cards may not be personal, the sentiments are often worth our attention. So, to all my readers: may you enjoy peace and a spirit of generosity now and through the year—even toward that annoying guy in the cubicle next to you.

Wherever you work and whatever you do, be happy at the holidays. It can be a special time, even at work.

Holiday Homestretch

In a scene from an old children's movie, a young man who was having trouble at school rubbed a magic lantern with his most fervent request: "I wish every day was Christmas or Saturday." For many of us, those days mean no school and no work.

Christmas week is a time when work seems to matter less. And everyone does work less. Half the world is already on vacation and the other half is on Facebook while they are supposed to be working.

It can be a time to catch up, it can be a time to make plans for the new year, and it can be a time to recover from a year of working hard. It can be a time to be productive or to get to know the guy you work with who has not taken his earphones off all year.

In all cases, enjoy the time; it only comes once a year.

The Giving Dilemma

As if the holidays don't have enough stress, every year we have to decide what to do about gifts for others at work. The potential issues are mind-boggling.

What is too much or too little?

What is too personal? Forget anything in a Victoria's Secret box.

What if my coworkers are Jewish or Muslim?

What if there is an office swap and I cannot find anything for under $10?

Then, there's the boss...

What's a proper gift if I hate him? Or if he hates me?

What if he thinks it's a brownnose gift? If my boss gets me a gift, do I have to get one for him?

Then there is that woman in the cube a few rows over who I like. Should I get a gift for her?

These are all very complex questions, and the way you answer them can affect your career, your future, heck, maybe your family's future! All because of a holiday gift.

Better keep some wrapped boxes of chocolates hidden under your desk.

Is It Total Stress or Long Lunches over the Holidays?

I have discovered two kinds of people at work each December.

The first is that group who appreciates that the world is slowing down. They *could* make more sales calls and work hard but there is no one home on the other end. So they relax, take longer lunches, and get ready to hit it hard in January.

The other group is made up of those who work even harder in December. There are books to be closed, plans to be made, and taxes to be filed. This group dreads December because it's all about grinding it out over long hours.

Each group watches the other with apprehension.

Most of us fall between the two groups and are thankful for that. Stressed or relaxed, December has a hint of goodwill and peace to all in the spirit of making the organization just a little better.

Who can argue with that?

To Deliver or Not to Deliver, That Is the Question

For those who work, getting to the mall during the holidays is akin to looking forward to a root canal. Plus, there is too much to do for the year-end at work and it's just too crowded at the mall. The alternative is appealing and easy, so we get busy on our computers, and order and order and order.

And the question becomes, where do we want all that stuff delivered? The logical choice is to have it delivered at home. But since we are at work, do we want packages hanging around on the front porch all day? And what if a signature is required?

Should we get the orders delivered to the office? What is the policy on that? Do we really want coworkers to see what gifts we are buying? Could be awkward.

Online shopping is increasingly the way of the world for busy people at work. But when it comes to some gifts and deliveries, maybe the mall isn't as bad as we thought.

The Stress of Holiday Cards

The decision-making stresses of the holidays could fill a long list. Whether or not to send holiday cards to coworkers is on the list. I like receiving cards but the sending thing is another story, and raises a long list of questions.

There's that guy in the cubicle next door who sings "Uptown Funk" all day. Does he deserve a card? Will he think I like him?

If I send a card to the boss's home, will she think I am a stalker? How will I get her address?

What if I can't get the cards out until after Christmas? Will I seem like a slacker?

Does an e-card count? Is "Season's Greetings" too impersonal? Who celebrates Christmas and who doesn't?

Should I only send a card to those who sent one to me?

The easy way to eliminate stress is to make it easy. Send a card with warmest greetings to all.

And Goodwill to All

Some would claim that the holidays are all about being nice to others. I agree. In that spirit, I suggest that holiday cheer extend to our coworkers. Impossible? No! Just a few more civil acts can create peace on earth and goodwill toward men, or at least make the workplace just a little better.

To name a few:

Wash your dishes or put them in the dishwasher in the office kitchen. Yes, you know who you are if you are guilty.

Don't take the newspaper from the lobby into the bathroom. Disgusting!

Talk to your colleagues—don't e-mail or text them if they are right next to you.

Introduce yourself and be nice to the temp worker who is scared to death that each day is his last day.

Tell people outside of your usual circle that they did a great job.

The goodwill thing can make us all a little better at work.

Three Ways Halloween Can Kill Your Career

Halloween at work is now almost as risky as the annual holiday party. As Halloween has grown in popularity, so have the risks of celebrating a little too much. Before you write a comment, please know I enjoy Halloween as much as anyone. Walking around in the evening and watching the excitement on children's faces is always fun. It's the adults in the office who cause me worry.

Each year, Halloween grows in its impact on the workplace. Although unofficial, it is now a day of celebrating and dressing up in almost all workplaces. It can be a day when both personal judgment and organizational rules are suspended. On a diet? Go ahead and have that Snickers anyway. Productivity? Not today. No dogs allowed in the office? The dogs can run around on Halloween, as long as they are in costume.

Halloween is not a big holiday everywhere. I know lots of people who are not even sure Halloween *is* a holiday for adults. And many are sure that it is not one to be celebrated at the office. And in many places outside of the U.S., it is a nonevent. But here we are, about to celebrate it again. Ask any zombie, ghoul, or clown, and you will hear thousands of ways that Halloween can hurt your career. In my experience, they can be boiled down to three killer categories. Here they are: three ways Halloween can kill your career, with a few guidelines to keep you out of the trap.

1.   Dressing up like a bumblebee. It doesn't have to be a bumblebee—any costume that will set you up for humiliation is a killer. One year not long ago, I saw the EVP of finance at a Fortune 500 company prance around all day in a bumblebee costume. He had a great time but he never regained the respect of the department. Some images tend to stick. There is no time when others' perceptions of you take a day off. If you are up for a promotion, this rule is all the more important. If you are in a position of authority, dress up accordingly.

The converse is true also. Don't make fun of the boss. Don't dress up as the boss. It may sound like a good idea to you and your coworkers, but the boss may or may not have a sense of humor.

2. Dressing up like a French maid. It doesn't have to be a French maid—any costume that shows questionable judgment is dangerous. Any costume that borders on poor taste or is offensive is weird in the office, will be long remembered, and can kill your career. Wearing too little is definitely in that category. I know of an analyst at an investment banking firm who dressed up as a French maid and never recovered. No Puritanical judgment here, but sexy nurses, sexy zombies, and sexy Homer Simpson are all inappropriate for the office.

I shouldn't have to mention this, but anything that can be interpreted as racist, sexist, antigay, or otherwise offensive is just plain stupid. Mental patients, priests, nuns, and ethnic stereotypes might fit into this category. If you have to ask, the costume is out of bounds and should be tossed in the trash.

3. Getting drunk and then dressing up like a bumblebee or Miley Cyrus. Anything mentioned in numbers one and two is only made worse after a few drinks. The killer accelerator works when drunk and in an offensive costume.

Is Halloween just for kids to have fun dressing up and trick-or-treating? Or is it a time to have fun and show your coworkers your creative side? It's probably both. And why not have a little candy and celebrate instead of same old, same old, so have the Grouchy glasses handy. It's just those costumes and the adult beverages that can linger.

Just remember, in a day dominated by video, Halloween could be a holiday that comes back to haunt you and kill your career.

The Halloween Hangover

I've noticed that Halloween has a lingering effect in the office. The lingering is in the form of candy.

We want our children to go out trick-or-treating and to have fun. We just don't want them to enjoy the fruits of their efforts in the form of candy.

So all those Butterfingers and 3 Musketeers bars end up in the office in a big, tempting bowl. Somehow, it is okay to feed all our coworkers the food that we think is too unhealthy for our children. Worse, we eat it. Food we would never consider acceptable is okay right after Halloween.

Maybe it's a productivity trick. Maybe the bosses bring those Snickers bars in to give us that afternoon jolt. Or maybe it's a good mental bridge into casting diet decisions to the wind as the holidays approach.

Maybe it's why even adults like Halloween. Enjoy it.

Will You Be Mine?

Valentine's Day is now a tricky holiday at work. The impact Valentine's Day has at work is now approaching that of Halloween and St. Patrick's Day. And what to do on that day is just as confusing.

Is Valentine's Day a day to bring in chocolates for everyone? Or should I just ignore it?

What if I receive a mystery valentine? Did everyone receive one? Should I ask?

Is it a day to tell my coworkers I love them all even if I really don't?

Should I get dressed up in case something romantic happens?

What if something racy happens?

Valentine's Day is no different from other holidays at work. Good advice is to take a cue from the other holidays, use your good judgment, and never get drunk.

As one romantic friend exclaimed, "Productivity be damned, we need a holiday this time of year." Valentine's Day might be just another day—unless you finally act on that crush you have on the person in the cube next door. But, wait, maybe every day at work can be a little special.

My dad is ninety-two years old and he loves wine. When he receives a good bottle as a gift, he is always thankful and claims, "I am going to save this for a special occasion!" I want to say, Dad, at ninety-two, every day is a special occasion. He knows every day is special and that is my message to you, dear workers of the world.

There are some special occasions but, by and large, work is about making every day a little special.

Back to School Again

When summer camps are over, when family vacations are over, when the stress of the "who had the best vacation" contest is over, it must be time to go back to school. But wait, you are not in school anymore (but probably wish you were). The excitement of a new school year is only a memory. September is just another month. Instead of making new friends you are with all the same coworkers you have been with all year. Instead of picking new, exciting classes, you are picking which projects you are trying to avoid. Instead of a new wardrobe, you are still wearing the same things. Not to worry, there is at least one element from "back to school" that will continue to serve you well—planning.

For some, when the kids go back to school, it means it's time to return to a welcome routine. The kids are back in their routine, so let's do the same thing. But that's the problem. Don't just "settle" back into that routine.

For those without the kids and the stress of school drop-offs, the same "settling" could happen nonetheless. In fact, what I sometimes see, especially among people early in their careers, is a genuine wistfulness in September. There can be a sense of "wish I was back in college." September comes and goes, and we hope to avoid feeling depressed.

As the president of a college, I see the genuine sense of renewal that a new school year can bring. In part, it can be a time of such a feeling because the slate is clean. As the school year begins, no one is failing (yet), no one is on probation (yet), and anything is possible and all is good. It is a time for planning and goal setting.

I have discovered that most of us, regardless of our occupation, work on the academic calendar, so the beginning of the school year is a better time than January 1 for setting goals and resolutions for the new year.

The holidays are too cluttered and busy for thinking ahead. Plus, everyone is too tired for ambitious resolutions. Enter the academic year. That's when you are renewed from the restful summer and can set goals for the final quarter of this year and thereafter.

Go ahead, make some new year's resolutions now. It's the best time.

Those Summer Schedules

A key workplace question is this: Is Friday the new Saturday? Or, put another way: Am I the only one working on Fridays?

Traffic is lighter on Friday mornings.

But the traffic out of town at noon on Friday is jammed.

The lines at Starbucks are shorter on Fridays.

Fewer meetings are scheduled, which is always good. There are fewer e-mails in the box, and those out-of-office notifications pile up in e-mail on Fridays.

Oh, I forgot, Friday is the day when lots of people work from home. That must be why the beaches are crowded with people on their laptops.

I am all for holidays and long weekends, but it seems casual Fridays changed to no-work Fridays. If Friday is the new Saturday, I wish someone would resend me the memo.

When to Play Hooky

Some events dwarf the importance of work. Moon landings, presidential inaugurations, and any number of personal events and news command our attention in ways that time in a cubicle never can.

But what about those in-between events like the local team winning the World Series?

Based on the attendance at parades for any championship team, they are all events worthy of hooky. In a quick but very scientific survey of cubicle dwellers, all believed there were quite a few events worthy of hooky.

Holiday shopping was at the top of the hooky list, followed by birthdays, St. Patrick's Day, Valentine's Day, Groundhog Day, and the-kids-might-be-sick day. All very worthy hooky targets.

In fact, based on my scientific survey, the list of reasons to play hooky from work was, well, infinite.

Who am I to argue with science when it comes to hooky?

It's Super Bowl . . . Monday

Super Bowl weekend is a little oasis in the dark days of winter. It's a long game with long commercials and a long party. But wait, the Super Bowl is NOT just about Sunday—it goes on through Monday, and there are real workplace implications.

Separate surveys conducted by employment-information websites Glassdoor and Kronos Incorporated show that Americans are more likely to waste time or call in sick on the Monday following the Super Bowl than any other day of the year.

The Workforce Institute estimates that 4.4 million employees more than usual will come to work late. The survey further shows that absences related to the Super Bowl are especially high among young adults.

Since revelers are finding the Monday after the Super Bowl particularly hard to manage, there is a movement starting to make post–Super Bowl Monday a national work holiday.

And as a 49ers fan, I say, why not?

Celebrate St. Patrick

Let's bring St. Patrick's Day into the workplace. No, not the way you are thinking. Contrary to what some believe, St. Patrick did not invent alcohol and he wasn't known for overimbibing. He is known for driving the snakes out of Ireland. So let's bring the spirit of St. Patrick into the office and drive out the snakes.

Although there probably aren't literal snakes, there are plenty of reptiles at work you might want to drive out. How about driving out wasting time and jerk bosses? How about driving out too much stress for too little reward? How about driving out working all the time instead of enjoying what is important? How about driving out those snacks that give you bad breath?

March 17 each year is a time to celebrate all things Irish. So let's bring a little Irish into the workplace and make it a wee bit better.

A Final Word

Maybe figuring out the new workplace is not as hard as we make it. Maybe success is no further than a recall of lessons we learned long ago. Employee manuals are huge and rarely read. Guiding principles that hang on walls are pabulum and they all say the same thing about integrity and equality. All good, but there are a few simple rules we learned in high school that apply to the world of work today. Yes, high school.

1. Be home when you promised. Or, at work, always live up to what you promised.
2. Leaving a message doesn't mean you have permission, especially when it comes to spending money.
3. Let someone know where you are all the time. All the time.
4. If you're in trouble, don't negotiate.
5. In all cases, whatever you do, you will get caught. It just may be a matter of time.

Sounds simple, but like most simple rules, they are not always easy to follow, especially at work.

Acknowledgments

Many are those who contributed to the idea and completion of this book. Almost all had no idea that they had a hand in *The Thing About Work*. Thanks to all those who scheduled unnecessary meetings and conference calls. The time spent in those meetings allowed me to outline the book. Thank you to all the airlines and the barrage of delayed flights that allowed me to write. Thank you to all those I see in the workplace who are doing their best. Thank you to those who share their stories about work. Thanks to the family, the Menlo College family, and all those I have worked with along the way. You are all an inspiration.

Notes

1. Dawn Burke, "Hipster Bias: Another HR Hurdle?" *Fistful of Talent* blog, May 10, 2013, http://fistfuloftalent.com/2013/05/hipster-bias-another-hr-hurdle .html.
2. Steve Denning, "Think Your Job Is Bad? Try One of These!," *Forbes* online, August 11, 2011, http://www.forbes.com/sites/stevedenning/2011/08/11/think-your-job-is-bad-try-one-of-these/.

About the Author

RICHARD A. MORAN is president of Menlo College in Atherton, California. His career has included serving as venture capitalist and consultant to Fortune 500 companies as well as being active in the education community in Silicon Valley and beyond. As an evangelist for organizational effectiveness, he has authored seven best-selling books and is credited with starting the genre of "Business Bullet Books" with *Never Confuse a Memo with Reality*. His clients have ranged from Apple Computer and News Corporation to Silicon Valley startups and he derived lessons and humor from all. He is a frequent speaker on workplace issues, a frequent contributor and Influencer on LinkedIn, and hosts a weekend radio show on KCBS called *In the Workplace*.

Also by Richard A. Moran

Never Confuse a Memo with Reality

Cancel the Meetings, Keep the Doughnuts

Beware Those Who Ask for Feedback

Fear No Yellow Stickies

Nuts, Bolts, and Jolts

Sins and CEOs

Tweets, Feats, and Deletes